FIGHT

FIGHT

everything you ever wanted to know about ass-kicking but were afraid you'd get your ass kicked for asking

EUGENE S. ROBINSON

HARPER

An Imprint of HarperCollinsPublishers
www.harpercollins.com

HarperCollins books may be purchased for educational, business, or sales promotional use. For information, please write: Special Markets Department, HarperCollins Publishers, 10 East 53rd Street, New York, NY 10022.

FIRST EDITION

Designed by Ken Tabinsky

Library of Congress Cataloging-in-Publication Data is available upon request.

ISBN: 978-0-06-118922-7
ISBN-10: 0-06-118922-7

07 08 09 10 11 ID/RRD 10 9 8 7 6 5 4 3 2 1

An extension of this copyright page appears on page 211.

FOR ALL OF MY ENEMIES.

Every single one of them. Without you none of this would have ever been possible.

THE REAL & TOTALLY MIGHTY
TABLE OF FRIGGIN' CONTENTS

FIGHT

INTRODUCTION

FIGHTING: WHY NOT?

There's the spastic flurry of hands and the smell that always ends up smelling like chicken soup gone bad (fear). There's the mumble and the groan and eventually the slip into recognized roles (doer and done to). And finally, if everything works right, there's the reminder that we are far worse/better than the animals we own as pets and unsophisticated chattel.

What we are, though, is this: We are fighters.

And the scenario is repeated again and again. It wheedles its way into boardrooms and bedrooms, this not so particularly male obsession with the eternal, unasked "Can I take him?" Which could be extended to "Can I take it?" Or better yet, "Can I?" With all apologies due to Sammy Davis Jr. (also a student, despite his diminutive frame, of the fistic arts), the answer is always the same: "Yes I can." Even when you can't.

My name is Eugene. (Hi, Eugene.) And I'm a fightaholic.

"Hey, I'm going to need my seat back." The speaker was Todd Hester, former longtime editor of *Grappling* magazine, once editor of *Bodyguard*, and probably soon-to-be editor of an as-yet-unnamed mag. (Here's a scoop: *Ready2Rumble*—you didn't hear it here first). He's 6'4", 245 pounds. The scene was ringside at the very first King of the Cage competition, California's own paean to pummel. The year was 1998.

This was the response: "You're also going to need to breathe." The speaker was Rickson Gracie, one of the best fighters on the face of this *entire planet*. Probably any other planet you can think of. And there it is again, the skin torn off all of our quiet and civil discourse, civilly delivered but definitive in its assertion to your unasked question: "No. No, you can't. Not today. Maybe not ever (take me, that is)."

Or better yet, just simply, "Fuck no."

Because even though he's got two arms and two legs and a head just like you, there's no chance. None.

Hester apologized, grabbed his bag, and found a seat somewhere else. Laughing, he added, "Well I *did* need to breathe."

We *all* need to breathe. Some realize that sooner, some later. But of the ones who realize it, there are those whose realization of it does nothing to actually help them. Continue breathing, that is.

It started for me with another not-so-simple, simple question: "What the fuck are you looking at?"

It's New York City. The Clash's *Rude Boy* is letting out of a midnight showing in Bay Ridge. Three *cugines*—think Italian *cholos*—are fighting with three men by a gypsy cab. Two of the Italians have wrenches. One, curiously enough, in an Axis level of think-tank thinking, has a German shepherd. I am on the other side of the street. Crossed the street to get closer, natch, just as one of the be-wrenched cuginos took out the back window of the cab, which went skidding off into a Brooklyn night, leaving three very angry men with no reasonable resolution to whatever situation was at hand.

"What the fuck are you looking at?"

It was times like these that were meant for words like *fracas*, *melee*, and *donnybrook*. Broken bottles, broken noses, broken jaws ensue, and at the end of it I ended up in an emergency room with my left lower earlobe dangling and cartilage torn inside my ear. Topographical maps of the evening's fun had spread out all over my suit in bloodied rivulets. I cleared my throat and waited for the overweight and angry nurse to render assistance because, after all, this was an

EMERGENCY. "Yeah, yeah, they're *all* emergencies," she said. And aside from the guy who walked in smoking a cigarette to announce that he had been shot (and he had, right in the thigh), we all had to sit and ponder the highly ponderable foolishness of our wayward ways.

It was a meditation that inevitably carried me along with it back to the crawl space at home, where—in my head—I had already retrieved my Hi-Standard pump-action shotgun. Except, you see, it's not so easy to stroll through the kitchen with a pump and a bloody suit when you're seventeen in a household where people give even the remotest fuck about you. Back at the hospital, I got stitches and a meditation that stuck. If I was going to do this shit, I might as well learn to do it right.

"This is called the rear naked choke," said Matt Furey.

I was standing at AKA Kickboxing in San Jose, California. Now it's the home of a revolving group of at least eight great fighters of significant worth; names you'll never even know—well, all right, if you must know, Dave Camarillo, Bob Southworth (Frank Shamrock used to work out there), Phil Baroni, Josh Thomson, Paul Buentello, Mike Swick, Mike Kyle, and owner Javier

Mendez. But back in 1999, it was where NCAA champion wrestler Matt Furey reigned. Though now widely derided by those in the know as sort of a quasi–Billy Blanks exercise enthusiast, Furey was (and is) the real deal. I'd seen his Charles Atlas–esque ad in some weekly rag, and where it said, "Want To Fight?" I thought, Yeahhhh. And so after eight years of kenpo karate ("You might as well have been studying interpretive dance"), a year of muay thai, and a month of thinking about how another Gracie (Royce this time) had run through the competition in the first bow of what's now called mixed martial arts, no-holds-barred or submission fighting, I wanted to learn the rear naked choke. I mean, Gracie won using this selfsame choke—I had to learn it.

But what do you do when they get you in one of these?

"That's like asking, 'What do you do after you've been knocked out?'" said Furey.

Dream?

No. Not yet. But to hell with this brain-twisting Mr. Miyagi crap. Patience is not a virtue I'm given over to, and so off with the Eastern aphorisms, barroom wisdoms, and—how about just this: field-testing. Screw the books, bring on the left hooks. What say we bounce?

Bounce?

Bounce. Not the intransitive slang verb but, you know, more Patrick Swayze-in-*Road House* bounce. It seemed so seemly, what with me now pushing the scales at 265 pounds of animal under my skin, that, of course, I should end up here: here being floating raves, stripper security scenes with me wielding Maglites and escorting mud wrestlers amidst and betwixt fucking bachelor parties full of drunken hockey players, or South Bay clubs where those who came to fuck but didn't would stay to fight.

It was like a dream. You could even say it was dreamesque. And I was The Bouncer With The Groovy Demeanor. Also known as The Choker. Also known as Mr. Clean. And despite being in Fight Heaven, I was dour. Daily. Because, you see, commerce had sullied the waters. I *liked* to fight but I was being *paid* to work.

And work I did.

Witness: He asks her to dance, she says *no* after giving him the loser scan, and he, maybe not so predictably, loses it. Punches her down to the floor. In life I'm quite sure things will never get better than this for this man. I throw him and his brother out of a double door, one of which is locked. They hurl invective from beyond the safety threshold, the doorjamb of justice.

"Fuck you, fuck you, fuck you, fuck you."

"Anything else?"

"Yeah, fuck *you*."

And that was it. Five fuck-yous is one fuck-you over my fuck-you limit. I step across the doorjamb. His friend, who's been hiding behind the closed door, punches me in the face and as I turn to get him, Fuck You Man punches me in the face. Like some Popeye cartoon my head swivels with each hit until I figure out that first things must come first. So I choke out—rear naked choke out—Fuck You Man while his friend works on my head from behind. Then I turn to him and choke him out, and the police show up with guns drawn and haul them away.

Invigorated? Not exactly. Because though the fight is joy enough on its own, it wasn't enough. I had to write a report for the manager describing what happened.

"What happened is my jaw hurts and I should probably get some fucking X-rays."

"What's *going* to happen is that you'll finish writing that report and then go chew some fucking gum because we can't afford X-rays."

Now the water was muddied as muddied could be. My jaw was fine but I was pissed off. And the next night, as I stood between The Two Guys and The Three Guys apparently scheduled to fight The Two Guys, I started to wonder what it was all about, Alfie. And right about that time there was a looping overhand from The Three Guys and I knew what it was about. It wasn't about *stopping* fights. I mean I wasn't here for *that*. That'd be like a hooker working a Mormon ministry in a massage parlor. I was here to fight. Specifically, to protect my still-throbbing jaw from all sorts of chewing-gum-related HMO concerns.

So I trapped the sloppily delivered punch and began punching the puncher in the mouth, always the offending mouth, the savage jaw. I was grabbed by guy number two of The Three Guys, and I swiveled my arm under his arm and into a hip throw that landed him on the ground, where I stomped and stomped until guy number three tried to take me down. I grabbed his hair and began working an anvil chorus of his head against the marble bar against the rising chorus of screams and shouts, now all in unison . . .

"EUGENE, STOP! STOP! EUGENE, STOP! . . ."

Through the mist of all of the blood lusting, I did note that they were all calling *my* name. Curious. But not nearly so curious as them firing me. For fighting? Hahahahaha. Fuck them.

There are some places that *know* fighting, and so from Furey I went to Marcus Vinicius at Beverly Hills Jiu-Jitsu. I drove by it laughing. That was before I knew. It sort of seemed like Tough Guy Day Spa. Beverly Hills Jiu-Jitsu. Except it really was. Vinicius was training cats named Judo Mark, and training with Bas Rutten, Darrel Gholar, Mark Kerr, and Vin Diesel, for chrissakes. It was a who's who of asskickage. The crème de la concussion crème. Guys who, given the Mike Tyson archetype of big and burly, are not any kind of a guy who'd register on your street radar as giving off any kind of a nature's warning signal—unless you count cauliflower ears, or preexisting subdural hematomas, or cuts around the eye. The most dangerous men, man to man, in Los Angeles. Who'd a thunk it?

Sunk in off Robertson and not even gifted with anything more than a *half* number—912½ South Robertson—it looked much less like a strip-mall self-defense deal and much more like a place where if you didn't like to, want to, need to fight, well, you could just get the fuck out. All pea green outside and walls of blue pads inside, it recalled nothing for me if not New York's Gleason's, or one of those places in John Huston's *Fat City*. But in the early afternoon of a California white Wednesday, it was where I was going to be if being here meant I'd get to fight those guys who fought here.

"What are you doing?" Vinicius called me aside. "We're just *training* now. Not *fighting*. Don't be like Joe Charles."

There was a difference, it seemed. Training is what you do when you're getting ready to fight. Fighting was what I was doing. I had learned it from Furey. And Furey had learned it from Karl Gotch, one of the old-time greats whose steady stock-in-trade was a sort of studied and serious sadism so significant that at one time they had called that style of wrestling, "ripping." And Joe Charles had learned it from Judo Gene LeBell (see "Gotch, LeBell, Gable: The Holy Troika of True Tough," in chapter 8) and it was just a different way of being done and it was a way that guaranteed that if you learned anything, you'd learned it because you were a tough sonuvabitch.

And if you didn't learn, you'd go home hurt.

In football it'd have been called "unnecessary roughness," but there seemed to be something pretty necessary about it. I'd stay with Vinicius, barring hell or high water, because he's a technician's technician, but I'd never forget for a minute the taste in the mouth of that certain savagery, hinted at in classes, aggressively suggested in the streets. You see, that's really why I was there, because that's what it was that got me. Sure, I could train, and I did, but I really wanted to fight. Not sport-fight either (which is about as close as you can get), but *fight*. Not Ultimate Fight, but *fight*. Reliving like we do, perhaps, the burn of first loves, this love of the fight. I wanted to train but I *had* to fight.

Enter Oxbow.

Call it a pro-social umbrella for antisocial activity. Call it a band. Call it a couch whereby the id airs itself out and people, frequently *fans*, come to enjoy music. Call it a nightly excuse/invitation to be taken seriously when you ask: "Can I take him?" And, lest confusion sully the waters here, this has much less to do with the TV-coach trope of *winning* and much more to do with just fighting. Win or lose, I love it just the same.

Hold on. That's a lie. I like winning much more, but I like fighting enough to risk the losing because in the end it's the fighting that justifies itself and not the winning or the losing. Call it Zen and the Art of Kick Assertainment.

And they lined up in long lines: ice throwers, hecklers, critics, guys hiding by back doors, women trying to club me with beer bottles, stoner rock dudes with knives, wanting to go all Wide World of Nature on me and try their "luck."

And what's more, something else happened on the other end of business. Girls whose boyfriends had beaten them, dominatrixes who needed an edge on an increasingly demanding clientele, as well as art rockers and tattooists willing to trade for trade—twenty-four-hour party people started coming to me wanting some get-back, or at the very least to learn *how to* (see chapter 13, "I Killed a Man"). And add to that the fact that I had started making worlds collide, writing about fighting pros so that I could fight pros, who inevitably kicked my ass because they *are* pros—Daniel Gracie, Cesar Gracie, Frank Shamrock, Rico Chiapparelli out in Redondo—and you have a prescriptive for the cyclical nature of life.

They, the more skilled, beat me, the less skilled, savagely. I, in turn, would beat those less skilled savagely. With a soundtrack of unholy squall throbbing in clubs in Germany, England, or the Netherlands, or standing on the sidewalk club-side in Maine. Now, I don't mean to diminish Oxbow's art, and make no mistake about it, when *Vice* magazine called us "the best art rock band in the world," they knew whereof they spoke, but I do mean to underscore the symbiotic arrangement we have when, realistically speaking, critical accolades are not enough. We'd rather play a set than fight one, but in the end it's almost the same thing.

Then this from the record label: "We thought you might like this." It was, or would have been, had it been handwritten, a scribbled e-mail inducement to Fight Club. Rule Number One of Fight Club: Do not talk about Fight Club. But here it was. You had to call a number, and go to an address, and then buzz a buzzer, and meet a man named Hank before moving off to a cranky old elevator and into a room next to an incinerator with about twenty other dudes.

Perfect.

There are no referees here. Nothing but graying concrete, men who don't look at each other except in sidelong glances of appraisal, and heat pipes that raise the temperature, pre-fight, to a standing twenty degrees hotter than outside. Did I mention the smell of garbage that wafted through the place? This one was in San Francisco, but it's a movable feast, and it travels up and down the West Coast and it bows in Venice, San Jose, out in San Fernando for chrissakes. Pancrase guys from Hong Kong. Boxers coming in from Seattle. Stretching and taping their fists. I'm stretching and taping my fists. And after doing all of these things I find myself in a tight ring. It's tight to force faster action. Tight to discourage tourists. I'm faced off against a guy with a David Niven mustache. He's about 215 (to my now svelte, well-cardio'd and non-steroided 210). I kick his legs with Muay Thai kicks and he backs up and I'm back in Brooklyn again thinking, "Oh yeah. I CAN . . ." I bob. I weave. I drop my right hand.

I wake up on the mat.

He was a southpaw. He was also Chris Sanford, one of the stars of Spike TV's not-long-gone *Ultimate Fighter* show and a Cesar Gracie protégé (see chapter 16, "I Stoop to Conquer"). Funny thing about getting knocked out: it steals your time away. And the ten seconds you were down there while feeling like a blink paradoxically also have you feeling long-nap refreshed and saying shit like, "I tripped."

But moments like this were made for Memorex, and instant replay had shown me taking a solid one and falling to the mat. I shrugged, got the fuck off the mat, and knew something then that keeps me coming back to this basement, other basements, and fights that I win or fights that I lose, and that's: Our essence is divine, we are infinite, and I am going to try to kick your fucking ass.

"You had the weirdest light around you. And this smile on your face," my mom said. I was seventeen. You see, some kids' moms were drudges, Florence Henderson martyrs of motherly attentions. Mine, all Diana Ross cool, was stepping between me and three bouncers at The Ritz, New York City, New York, minutes before a Killing Joke show and minutes before I was going to be tossed bodily down a flight of marble stairs. The fight had been short and set up, and with my arms pinioned behind me and three of them, it was soundly, squarely, nay, healthily one for the L column. "You seemed really very, very content. It was strange."

Do tell.

BIG IRISH JOE DONNELLY, MY SHRINK, ASKS A FEW QUESTIONS IN A THINLY VEILED ATTEMPT AT SEEING IF HE'S GOT THE STONES TO TAKE ME ON

We know you like to fight, but why?

Short answer? It's expressively honest. There's no real equivocation in an elbow to the jaw, no pussyfooting about the gray shadings of meaning inherent in civilized and power-shielded discourse. And it's a potent tie to our immediate and ever-present animal. Now, words are all well and good, and like the Meat Puppets say, "Well, who needs action" when you got words, but in a land where words have ceased having meaning, this will have to do. Nicely. The problem here is, largely, this has become *the* model for our national discourse. In other words, fighting has become trendy. Not the stuff in the ring, which I will love no matter what, but the idea that words are an embarrassment used only by those who do not know how, can't, or are afraid to fight. Remember, I *choose* to fight and I do so not because I have no other choice but because it's frequently, in the wide and rainbowed palette of personal expressions, the expression that people seem to most want to see.

So my reasons for wanting to fight are:

Part Florence Nightingale: It's not unusual for me to be *thanked* by the beaten. If not right away, then later. I'm not a bully and only fight as a last recourse, and if it's some ass clown who's been pushing and pushing, well, he's thanking me for teaching him a lesson as gently as a hardhead like him is likely to notice.

Part Ted Bundy: Vast wellsprings of rage, the sources of which go back to early-life Freudian shit having everything to do with every single existential and psychosexual issue you can ever imagine. Not to politicize my way around this, but I've got a very, um, very complicated relationship with other human beings.

Part Zorba the Greek: I like to fight.

But what about the moral and legal repercussions?

If you are a reactive fighter, not a bully, the law affords you a good deal of latitude. I mean, under the rubric of *defending* yourself you can get away with murder. Literally. Also, being well dressed, sober, and articulate can be a great saving grace and a license for the aforementioned murder. I was at this party, trying to make my way through the crowd to get out. The police were breaking things up. A biker stood in my way. I said, "Excuse me." He belched. I walked around to the left. He stepped in front of me. I walked to the right. He walked to the right. I looked at him and said, "I'm going to give you until the count of three to get the fuck out of my way. One . . . two . . ." (Always go ON the number three, please.) I broke his nose and shattered his cheekbone with three solid right crosses that put him down, as luck would have it, right at the feet of the cops, who asked me what happened. Well, I looked at the unconscious biker, drunk, covered in blood and beer; I looked at the cop and said as honestly as possible, "He fell." Good enough for the cop who arrested . . . HIM . . . on the spot. This covers the legal ramifications.

As for moral ramifications? None to speak of that I know about. I mean, to quote AC/DC, "I never shot nobody that didn't carry a gun."

I mean, sure, sure, you cry a few crocodile tears if you're around a woman who you like and you want a few extra-special points for Alan Alda–esque sensitivities and a certain amount of noble savagery. The reality, though? It's as fun as the most fun thing you could ever do. Crushing your enemies, driving them before you and hearing the lamentation of their women? It doesn't get much better than this. (My apologies to John Milius for that.)

Is this what your teacher, Marcus Vinicius, taught you?

Marcus Vinicius is one of the greatest men and fighters that I know. He's a gentleman and in true Brazilian fashion would be shocked and appalled at my extracurricular application of a discipline that he reveres. He pursues the fight game globally. I've spent time with him in Russia and here. He's gone to Serbia, Italy, the Amazon rain forest, Japan, and Puerto Rico in search of the Apollonian heart of this Dionysus. While Marcus has taught me the finer points of Brazilian jiu-jitsu—a coterie of chokes, cranks, and debilitating arm bars—his South American mix of an easygoing love of life combined with a certain machismo made my distinctly North American assholishness something I necessarily had to leave at the door. But make no mistake, what he taught me, he taught me to great effect.

Translation: If I've choked you the fuck out, don't thank me. Thank the great Marcus Vinicius.

How did Oxbow become part band, part fight club?
Oxbow is *all* band, and if you were looking for four musicians more serious about playing the music they play, you couldn't find any. Serious. Pretentious. Portentous. It is not easy music to play. Unfortunately this means that in concert the *most important thing* for us is the *playing* of that music. Not the fact that you want to show your friends how funny it is to piss off the Negro with the knife on stage in his underwear by screaming shit at him that would get you largely the same treatment streetside *sans* the amps, the speakers, and all the rest. In any case, because disrespect seems to beget disrespect, if you don't want to hear the music and you don't want us to play the music we're being paid to play, well, it seems that leaves very little doubt as to what you really want: to get to know us better. Closer. More intimately. And you will.

But yeah, your instincts are right here. There was an evolution to this position. It occurred one night when a "friend" taunted us the whole show.

Because he was a "friend," we gave him a pass. But after the show it felt so bad, like we had failed as musicians *and* artists, that we decided to NEVER, EVER again ignore the reality of the moment. To never ignore the hereness and the nowness of this Zen two-step between you and us. And so it goes: We're engaged in the collective creation of a piece of art. It's as egalitarian as it gets. Everyone participates. For good or ill.

But the most important thing to note here is when playing a show, we'd always rather just finish playing the show than fight. (That is the collective WE.) And when fighting a fight we'd always rather just finish fighting the fight than play the show.

Can you beat me?
Beyond a shadow of a doubt.

GQ MAGAZINE & A FEAR & SICKNESS UNTO DEATH

Thom Gunn, former friend of the fistic arts, in some sort of San Francisco elegy made this point clear about fighting—specifically streetfighting. Far from being a Sam Peckinpah-ish ballet of orchestrated chaos, it was, he opined, except when practiced by a select few, graceless animal activity. Even worse than that: animal activity without the economy. A stumbling bumble of flailing fists, fatigue, and, at least half the time, failure.

Yeah, whatever.

Where Gunn saw our ridiculousness on display there are some who see, in the Science of the Balled Fist, the untold story of all of our stories, the key to God-Given Sex Appeal, and an archetype so thoroughly us that once said it just seems impossible that it even needed to be said in the first place. All hail The Ass Kicker.

The Ass Kicker, not-so-distant cousin of The Face Slapper, The Foot Puter Down-er, The Big Stick/Soft Talker, discredited in this present age of American exceptionalism but still so deeply ingrained in the Western methodology that you can see us all try to figure out why our John Wayne is not playing better with the natives.

But this ain't about that.

This is about Dionysus and the Joy of the Fight.

Flash to Trembling Voice on the Phone. "Well, there have been complaints."

Perfect. Complaints.

"It seems that there are many who are thinking that, um, fighting is not all that 'gentlemanly.'"

What about Marquess of Queensbury? *Dueling*, for chrissakes. It's nothing *but* gentlemanly. Steve Friedman, staffer at *GQ*, was explaining things to me. Specifically, how a nation was still searching for its testicles amidst all the men's fragrances and fragrant men's gewgaws, gimcrack, and doodads. The hubbub? My article on the newly emerging sport of the no-holds-barred Ultimate Fighting. Also known as Mixed Martial Arts. Also known as Extreme Fighting. Also known by Senator John McCain in his now famous broadside, as "human cockfighting."

The Fragrant Ones were questioning our bona fides as gentlemen.

RULE NUMBER 37: Never question another man's bona fides as a goddamned gentleman if you expect to walk away without a fight.

And like Carl Panzram, ye olde serial killer and mass murderer, once said, I wish they all had one neck and I had my hands around it. This is all about never wanting to walk away without a fight, and if there was anything that ever made anyone who liked to fight want to fight it was this idea that fighting is somehow a lesser impulse, urge, compulsion than . . . what? What on the great pyramid of basic and enduring activities was *above* fighting? Our entire Judeo-Christian tradition is based on unending struggle. When Jacob fought all night with an angel on the road to Judea, when wrestling is the only sport to appear in the *Iliad*, it's a damn sure sign that *GQ* will yield to my willful desire to do yet another article on the *mano* and the *mano* for their bespoke magazine.

"It seems that there are many who need their heads bounced off the walls like so many fuzzy, yellow tennis balls, you prick, you."

My name, and indeed any article on fighting, was forthwith destined never to grace the pages of *GQ* again.

So, this book. At once a tribute, a how-to guide, and a non-apologia for one of the world's most goddamned vital activities: the fight.

ONE
WHAT THE HELL ARE YOU LOOKING AT?
PART 1

Cities are great incubators for highly evolved animal behaviors. Jam thirty rats in a space better suited for fifteen rats and you have the same sort of churlishness that was an earmark of pre-9/11 New York, where in the 1970s-80s swelter of returning Vietnam vets, junk (and the junkies to go with it), punk rock, and disco. You could find a fight as easily as a randomly exchanged glance. Reckless eyeballing, different from its Jim Crow southern variant, took on a whole different meaning in my NYC *roman à clef*. While this is a monograph about fighting it's also the story of a fighter. As I stood on a sidewalk a block or so off of Eastern Parkway at a rundown park on the edge of Crown Heights, I knew what I was hearing even before I knew what to do with what I had heard.

What the hell are you looking at?

Depending on your age, disposition, race, socioeconomic makeup, half-empty-half-full outlook on life, and where you come from, you're liable to do any number of things at this here juncture in time.

You:

1. Keep on walking: Not such a bad option—if you're a priest. Or David Carradine in that TV show *Kung Fu*. It shows a remarkably adult take on separating that which is important in life from that which is not. It also shows that you're a non-confrontational puss.

Exceptions: When you're well dressed, in a hurry, and/or with a date. These three in concert, the perfect storm of Unlikely To Roll Around In The Dirt With Morons, when in evidence will also make you a prime target for morons. Like running from a large angry dog or not snorkeling in Florida swamps, no one will think less of you for doing this.

2. Act like you didn't hear anything: This is a mere variation on number 1. A more pathetic variation, incidentally.

3. Go nuclear: You know it's coming. And you know what the "it" is that's coming. Forget about doing any sort of meeting *halfway*. You know there's a point at which you figure out that your garbage disposal is not a spoon *washer* but a spoon *bender*, and that point could be now.

So you . . .

    a. Attack: Call it a preemptive strike. While this is much harder to defend in a court of law, in the eyes of the habitués of the street scene this sort of bravado is the stuff of legend.

    b. Start screaming: Animals do this all the time. It's a kind of mimicry and the thinking of those who study animals is thus: if I can convince this angry Puerto Rican that I am a rhino, he will be frightened. This may or may not work. Remember—duress constricts vocal cords. Constricted vocal cords can thrust you back to puberty. Is Urkel a tough rhino? No. No, he is not.

    c. Flee: While this clearly lacks any sort of couth at all, when combined with b) and even in odd cases with a), it makes for a bouillabaisse of semi-effective coping and survival strategies.

DRAWBACKS: You may still get your ass kicked. Savagely. By men with no appreciation for your theatrical tour de force. While summer stock may beckon, it'll have to wait until the bruises clear.

    4. Do what I did: Negotiate: The key to any successful negotiation is your ability to convince all and sundry that your willingness to go 3a) or 3b) is higher than their willingness to do the same. Moreover, since willingness is only part of the pie here, ability is a factor as well, so you best develop some ability or learn to mimic it. Ability mimicked badly will weaken your negotiating posture, as it makes an ass beating more than likely. But how do you negotiate your way around *What the hell are you looking at?*

    Easy peasey. The answer is: "YOU."

    Now his choices are highly limited: escalate, or decide that you are the bigger rhino and walk away. In my non-fictional rendering, however, he chose the former. Yes, he escalated by returning with the age-old and surprisingly useful *Oh yeah?* And like the rising hands on the baseball bat of one-upmanship this was spoken as he was closing the distance betwixt us, before he concluded that thought with *You like what you see?*

    Your turn. Escalate or de-escalate? Now, be careful here. This is the trickiest part of your negotiation as animal brains reign and even something said to de-escalate might get used to escalate.

    For example:

You say, *No, man. Forget it.*

He says, *So now there's something wrong with my face, fuckface?*

So if you're hellbent for escalation, like I was, you say something like what I said when I said, *I don't know WHAT I'm seeing.* There's a certain genius to this line. Or at least as much genius as a ten-year-old is likely to be able to bear. The genius comes from the fact that you have now said something confrontational, but *confusingly* confrontational. It's the functional equivalent of telling a girl when she asks you if those pants make her look fat: "Fat's the least of your troubles, baby."

So now he was facing me, I was facing him, and it was looking like a draw. Almost *exactly* like a draw, in fact. Yes, a draw right up to the very moment that he bliztkrieg'd my face with several well-placed blows thusly concluding our lesson and my failed attempt at negotiating a fruitful settlement.

Now, what went wrong?

The sage observer will recall Tuco from *The Good, The Bad & The Ugly*: "If you're going to fight, fight. Don't talk." So here begins the cavalcade of wrong: letting any angry person get too close, trying to debate a moron, and finally, hoping for the best on a planet where that's the least likely thing to happen. What the hell was I thinking?

Well, I wasn't. And that's the deal here—not thinking. In a place where not thinking is largely going to be more effective than thinking, not thinking doesn't mean NOT KNOWING. I wasn't thinking, and that was fine. Not knowing? Well, that was inexcusable.

So at this remove of years, 3,000 miles, and a Wizard of Oz–like hunger to know that which had previously been hidden, I decamped to the unlikeliest of places—a small, sleepy, beach community. A small, sleepy, beach community whose streets, based on my previous visits here, were filled with young men in late-model muscle cars who when asked for directions to the beach would gladly lean out of their passenger windows, going over and above the call of their now high-speed duty, to attempt to use ballpeen hammers to drive the point home that the only kind of California Dreaming you'd be likely to find in Huntington Beach is the kind you find when they get their heaping helpful fists of fury on you.

Yes, Huntington Beach, California. To meet the Wizard. In this instance, the original Huntington Beach Bad Boy, a handle hung on him when straight from a six-month lockup for assaulting a cop's kid on the streets. He was then dragged, Rocky-style, into the Ultimate Fighting Championship, where people expected this barroom brawler to lose to "seasoned martial artists." His name:

Tank Abbott. Or the way he spins it. . . . "A-double B-O-double T . . . twice the man you'll ever be."

Twenty-seven seconds into his first cagefight, after he had knocked his four-hundred-pound opponent into a state of near paralysis, the boast didn't seem nearly so empty. He had been doing the same thing in bars up and down the boardwalk for years.

THE BAR, THE ROOM, THE BRAWL, TANK ABBOTT'S TRICKS ON HOW TO AVOID FINDING YOURSELF WAKING UP MORE THAN ONCE A DAY

"Oh, he deserved it." Tank's arm bent back and he drew on his first vodka of the day. Or at least the first one that I've seen. Vodka with a strawful of cranberry juice. The "he" in this instance, the "he" that Tank was speaking of wasn't any kind of universal "he." No. It was the cop's kid, the beating of whom had landed Tank in the slam.

"I was driving my truck around one night and got into it with this kid. I'm just trying to get somewhere and he's screaming 'Come on, Fatso. I'll kick your fucking ass if you get out of that truck.' I get out of the truck and he starts running. So I get back in the truck and fake him out as he's running BACK to my driver's-side window and he's flipping me off as he thinks I'm about to get back in but I get him and knock him on to Queer Street. But, yeah. His father was a cop and so in I went. I had had ten other run-ins, but I'd never gotten any time for it, but this time, even though I'd say it was just a streetfight, his father coached him through two or three story changes and so I was gone. Six months."

No prison shower-room problems?

Tank's eyes narrow as he takes full measure of my smirking face. "Nah. They don't want to fight in county."

The bar where we're sitting is notably upmarket. Huntington Beach has changed from the ballpeen hammer days in all but spirit. We're sitting ensconced in the red-tile, adobe-ized interior of a kind of place you imagine having dollar-drink nights on Jimmy Buffet's birthday. Tasteful. Good food, music and vibe. Not a place where you're likely to catch too many fights, but here's RULE NUMBER 23 courtesy of Willie Dixon: You can't judge a book by looking at the cover.

Tank's shown up an hour late and credits/blames it on trying to look decent, as the night in question, that night being TONIGHT, he's been tapped as a special surprise guest for like 300 Marines in the grand ballroom at the Hyatt Regency. Marines from the 3rd Battalion. Call themselves the Thundering Herd. And are described as the BALLS of the Corp. And waving down his second vodka, Tank's involvement in said tribute to those who both manage to fight AND live is going to be more than worth the price of admission.

"Drinks for ALL MY FRIENDS!!!" His purposeful and knowing lift from the Bukowski-inked *Barfly* is not accidental and there is more than a little of the Bacchus-based poet in Tank. At six feet, 275 pounds with a 600-pound-plus bench press, the similarities perhaps end there.

"Oh, Tank's not stupid," says Todd Hester, editor in chief of *Throwdown* magazine. "Not by any stretch. But he makes it easy for people to forget."

"The fire that fueled me always was—what was that thing . . . that metaphor . . . or that car from that thing: the gray ghost?"

A dark horse?

"No. The idea's just that there's a lack of respect, and then respect. Because between the two, something's happened. They learned something."

What?

"They learned that I'm much better than they thought. Much better. I mean, in a bar fight you always have that element. Every single time. And it's either because they don't notice, don't care to notice, or notice the wrong thing. I used to stalk these guys." Tank's warming up into his fourth drink. "Yeah.

The steroid-bodybuilder types," and on cue one walks in: 265 pounds, 5 percent body fat, sleeveless T-shirt, tribal tattoos, goatee, and stunner shades. He's a movie star without the movie and his girl doesn't know any better, either.

"You see, these guys," he says nodding toward Mr. Olympia, "would pull into a spot with a lot of fanfare and I'd spot them and I'd start making my move. Edging closer. Until I'd be back-to-back with him . . . or somehow in his circle."

Is this where we get to the "he deserved it" part?

"Well, I'd be back-to-back with him or suddenly like in his space. And it wouldn't take long. A comment. A noise. And then they're . . ." and he's miming drunks' drinks changing hands, hands waving in full regaling, chests bumping, and his playing the anti-Wizard thing for all its worth, and after a particularly inopportune comment the also inevitable, "'Hey . . . why don't you fuck off?!?' And I'd be acting afraid. Or shy. And I'd be egging him on with a comment here and there and then they'd cross that line and it'd be over."

Lots of ways for it to be over. Name a few.

TANK'S FEW WAYS FOR IT TO BE OVER

1) Head Butts: "they're now illegal in mixed martial arts [MMA, what the Ultimate Fighting Championship is] competition but I never met a head butt I didn't like. Easy and effective."

2) Any fistic combinations of use: jabs, uppercuts, crosses, elbows.

3) Any combinations to go horizontal to take away the big man's advantages, as well as restricting the action to the floor, where eyewitness accounts gets blurry: "I get them on the floor and they can't get up."

"The great Karl Gotch once said, 'Bulls die on the floor,'" I offer.

Tank smiled. "Here they did."

And when it was over?

"Well, the gray ghost had shown that on this day they were going to learn something. Call it respect if you want to. I mean they learned that I wasn't whatever they had thought I was that got them where they were when they figured it out."

And that was? The floor?

"The floor."

Tank's a study in contrasts. Built well for chosen endeavor: smallish ears lying tight to his head, narrow eyes, a whole upper row of false teeth from the

second in a small spate of drunken driving accidents, false teeth that he takes out when he fights, looking like, with his Snuffy Smith beard, all of the SoCal kind of hillbilly he sort of is.

And so there is method to his madness, it seems. In a town that sports an airport dedicated to The Duke, John Fucking Wayne, there is a logical consistency that echoes AC/DC's line about "Never shooting nobody that didn't carry a gun." He was a goddamned public servant. Like a Batman or something.

But there was this other thing that I was looking for, and that was the animal anger that drove one to fight. It was a calling that became a job, but well before that, it started out as an emotional need. I felt it. I have felt it and in the middle of an early 1980s interview with Anton LaVey from the Church of Satan I tried to get him to touch on it, back when I thought it had something to do with evil. I asked him about three times in the guise of discussing evil and he said, "Okay. Evil is what doesn't feel good." And I asked again because I was talking about bloodlust and an emotional delight in domination. And he finally begged off, "Look, I'm an atheist." The implication being that this was just a con.

Okay. I got it.

So it was with Tank. The ground floor of WHY WE FIGHT he had to have had his finger on. A father that bounced basketballs off of his head? A castrating mother? All of the familiar Freudian tropes.

"Well, I had an older brother who played football, and my father was a rah-rah football type of guy. A tough guy. I started fighting when I was nine. Wrestling . . ."

Yeah yeah yeah. But what about the rising rage that bites when you fight, do you feel it anymore? Did you ever?

"Not in the ring. Not ever. Because that's business. And it's strategy. And technique. I mean if anybody I was fighting in the ring managed to get some sort of emotion out of me, it'd be a tough day at work for them. But, no, I never felt any sort of emotion there. In the streets, though? Well, that was totally different. Anger is an emotion but it wasn't always THE emotion, but it had to do with the gray ghost thing. Showing them that things ain't always like they seem. I was that punk rock kid. I remember being 135 at fourteen years old. And I remember being surrounded by the whole school. And I fought then . . ."

And so there it is: fighting TO SHOW THEM. That I know. I've felt that.

   And so what about now . . . after the nine Ultimate Fighting Championship (UFC) wins, the magazine covers, the girlfriend who's an ex-model, the cash, the celebrity, and the handshaking that doesn't stop while we sit and drink, with even cops who used to ARREST him coming up for some of the juice? If you've already shown them what is it that gets you to the fucking party anymore? Out of bed? Anything?

"Cash. In the ring, cash. And outside the ring? Nothing. I mean, the occasional guy who doesn't know who I am and wants to start something is usually wised up by some of his friends before it gets to where it's going. The guy who wants to tell me 'fuck you,' well, that won't even get me to put my drink down. I mean I really don't have anything to show them anymore since I've showed them all."

At the age of forty-one does this feel like you've lost something? I mean, what do you do if this has defined your personality for so long? I'm not asking him for him. I'm asking him for me.

"This." And he waves down vodka number eight. And then points to a Henny Youngman look-alike sitting behind us. Eighty-six years old. And drinking. "That."

And then on cue he turns and catches at the muscle boy movie star sitting on the patio. "Let's go sit outside." And we all laugh and laugh. And I say, "Let's." But before we get around to doing this, Tank's girl shows up. Thin and drawn high and tight, she occupies that space of former-ex-something or other. Model. Actress. New York party girl. Whatever. She nods in my direction, not as a hello but as a question to Tank: Who the hell is that?!?

"Oh. He's writing a book on fighting and fighters and wants to interview me."

This sits less well than I thought it might have and I start to beg off just to give them some alone time.

"Sit down." And when Tank says to sit down, well, you consider it. And he tries to mollify, cajole, cheer to no avail as the hours tick by and the drinks chug on through, and it's clear as clear can be that when she says, "OH! It's just allllllllll about TANK ABBOTT, isn't it?!?!" that this is going to end the only way it can. And my obligation, as any might exist anywhere at all, is just to be absent when she says, "Do you KNOW what he just ASKED me, TANK?!?!" Because this evening is cruising toward an ass-kicking.

And their fighting continues at the Hyatt Regency amidst the Balls of the Corp, and I've started drinking too at this point and am drawing hard looks from the Thundering Herd until some of them start to recognize Tank while his girl is whining about having been a model and how she's not just one of "TANK'S GIRLS" and how she deserves to have doors held open for her and Tank is neither angered nor exasperated, and when I ask how long they've been together he says, "Ten months. . . . and about ten more days."

And he's still drinking and she's still beefing, and when he walks out on stage to hand off the award to the returning hero, along with the Mayor of Huntington Beach, he was just supposed to pass it along but the Thundering Herd is thundering in recognition of him and eighteen vodkas later that mike is as good as his and he's on the stage hands raised while the crowd screams and he says, "I wish I could be over there with you guys . . . KILLING HADJIS!!!" And the crowd goes wild. Tank, waving, weaves back to his table, to his girlfriend, who turns her back to him, and to the fight, any fight, that will most clearly mark his place in space.

THE FIRST CINEMATIC NOTE OF CAGE FIGHTING THAT ALSO DID NOT FEATURE MEN CLAD IN TOGAS, SANDALS & THE TELLING SHEEN OF BABY OIL

Hard Times (1975) Directed by Walter Hill

The men are shirt-free. They raise their hands in what appears to be surrender while circling each other. Surrender until they open their hands. No weapons. No weights. No edge. They're surrounded by a cage. Chain link. And touts around the periphery scream and wave dollars.

Hard times, indeed.

But we've seen shadings of this in every cheap chopsuey flick up to and including Bruce Lee's bows and *Rambo*, but back in 1975 this was dangerous, and no less so with Walter Hill at the helm. He who would also direct *The Warriors,* and quasi-action flick fare in *48 Hours* and so on. But before he had become a director he'd been pulling duty on oil rigs, construction, and other places where a man might learn his way around the business end of a fist.

And in his gritty-in-a-way-that-nothing's-been-gritty-since-the-'70s flick, a potboiler of a story of Depression-era fisticuffs starring Charles Bronson, James Coburn, and a raft of characters that looked like they had actually spent some time cage-side, we saw some, albeit fake, no-holds-barred fighting—hooks, knees, elbows, and leg sweeps—shadows of which would only later emerge later in the very real mixed martial arts (MMA) in America of the 1990s.

TWO

LET'S GET IT ON

There was an almost reverential glee that colored discussions of Tyson in his prime. It approached the damn-near mythical, this perception that as Heavyweight Champion of the *World* he was the undisputed baddest of the badasses around. And despite the oft-asserted riposte, "Well, for that kind of money I'd fight him," from both armchair athletes and journeymen alike, there was no money where those mouths were and this unspoken half-truth went relatively uncontested.

Until the Ultimate Fighting Championship (UFC).

What *started* as a scheme cooked up by the many-numbered boys from Brazil known as the Gracies—a long-revered clan of jiu-jitsu fighters who had for years offered large sums of money to ANYone who could beat them—*ended* up making good on the male instinct to quantify quality and figure out once and for all, for those who cared, who were the best baddest men alive.

Like some crazy Wild West deal, fighters, tough guys, boxers, and bouncers from all over the globe convened in an eight-sided ring to settle the world's longest running bar bet. No rules, no time limits. The understanding was pure *Mad Max*: two men enter, one man leaves. While neither Tyson, nor indeed ANY boxer of significant stature, put it on the line by showing up, there *was* one representing the sweet science, a ranked heavyweight who outweighed the Gracie he faced by some sixty-five pounds. Said heavyweight glowered at the smaller man from across the Octagon.

Later, some twenty-eight seconds later to be exact, the fight was over. The stunned boxer barely limped out of the Octagon and it seemed like, for fans of mano-a-mano, the world had changed just a little bit. You see, mixed martial arts (MMA)—a Frankenstein monster of wrestling, jiu-jitsu, kickboxing, boxing, and karate had been born, and the Heavyweight Champion of the World now seemed like a quaint misnomer. What tough *used to be* and what it was *now* were very different things.

I mean, sure, there had been those P. T. Barnum attempts to mix the martial arts before. Ali fought Inoki back in the 1970s on network TV, with Ali trying vainly to put together combinations that worked, and Inoki rolling on the floor trying some sort of karate that most Americans had heretofore only seen in badly dubbed Saturday-matinee showings of *Fists of Fury* or *Five Fingers of Death*. But this was clearly *not* the ticket, especially when you witnessed how quickly the big money walked. Even Don "Only in America" King wasn't interested.

What a difference twenty years makes.

The first UFC was an unqualified success when it hit in the mid-1990s. Subsequent matches were filled to the brim with glitterati—from Dennis Rodman and Jim Brown (who later moved into doing color commentary for the UFC) to Joe Rogan from TV's *News Radio* (and, later, *Fear Factor*) and the strangely placed David Hasselhof and *Baywatch* entourage. All were drawn by the promise of full-contact fighting without the shadiness of boxing or the sham of pro wrestling. And America responded similarly—whether it was because it offered white men the briefest of opportunities to see a combat sport where white fighters still had a chance, or whether it was because it REALLY answered the king-of-the-hill question, pay-per-view went nuts. Blood on the screen was like blood in the water. And out came the sharks.

Lobbyists of various stripes at the behest of, some would say, Don King and Vince McMahon, the current market-cornerers on sports violence and entertainment, were tugging on the coats of their congressfolk, who were officially "appalled" at what was sound-bitingly referred to as "human cockfighting." Cable stopped carrying it, only a few southern states would license it, and pay-per-view was effectively stalled.

A West Coast ad rep for TCI cable who asked to not be identified stated that they were getting pressure from "back East on the grounds that the UFC was not suitable for family viewing and we were not to accept advertising from them."

"If you knew the difference between shit and Shinola," says Paul "The Polar Bear" Varelans, early UFC competitor, occasional Dennis Rodman running buddy, and former college football player who easily tips the scales at well over 300 pounds, "would you still really want the shit?" The powers that be weren't chancing it and continued the UFC witch-hunt. But despite all of the backroom dealing, something amazing happened.

Its rabid collection of fans and fighters prospered. On a circuit that includes Brazil's UFC cognates, Vale Tudo and Luta Livre, Saudi Arabia's Abu Dhabi Submission Fighting Tournament (sponsored by a sheik and recalling nothing if not Bruce Lee's *Enter the Dragon*), and Japan's Shooto and Pride fights (where winners swing some serious celebrity in Tokyo) not to mention a raft of imitators from the Extreme Fighting Championships and a whole amateur network of men whose desire is to measure their skill, their mettle, their MANhood—a new testing ground sprang up.

Noting that more people get hurt playing football, boxing, or skiing, MMA fighters ply their trade while smirking at the highly paid glory-boy boxers they claim are owned by HBO and the moneyed Vegas set, smirking because the bragging rights to toughitude clearly belong to them. With boxing's red-light-district status worsened by questionable rulings, underwhelming fights and more courtroom feinting than ringside slugging, and WWF and WCW seemingly the unrestricted province of people for whom sports entertainment is *not* an oxymoron, Mixed Martial Arts *Is* the Shit. And its fighters are, hands down, some of the toughest men alive.

Fast, furious, and too legit to quit, two of MMA's early shining stars and bona fide Hall of Famers were profiled: the estimable Kevin Randleman, who is still fighting out of Ohio's Hammer House (where the motto is "Ground and pound 'em), and Maurice Smith, a Seattle kickboxer whose easiness belies the fact that he's absolutely destroyed some of the sport's toughest before semi-retiring a few years ago.

Are you ready? *Are you ready?* Then let's get it on.

TWO BAAAAAAAADDDD MEN

Kevin with a "K"

Kevin Randleman, thirty-four, all frosted blond hair (his quicksilver fashion choices have seen the hair change multiple times according to his wildly changing whims) and 215-pound sculpted physique, had been touted as the newest phenom, the Dennis Rodman of the UFC. His mercurial post-fight pronouncements would do The Worm some justice. One week he's quitting, the next week he's fighting, the next he's getting busted for using performance-enhancing substances. Allegedly. I was warned by Eddie Goldman, the Howard Cosell of Mixed Martial Arts, that he'd be just as likely to beat me as talk to me.

All lies.

Randleman, father of two and family man, was unfailingly cordial, and this stood in stark relief to the images that flooded through my brain pan of him riding astride a competitor that he was beating into the "loss" side of the equation. Wrestling from the age of ten and going on to fight in the Golden Gloves, win the Big ten championships three times and the NCAA championships twice, Randleman was maxing in the twilight that eventually claims most of our top wrestlers. Teaching, training, coaching and waiting, until one day the phones rings and it's Mark "The Hammer" Coleman, president of Hammer House, former Olympian and once Randleman's Ohio State Coach, and he's asking the question to which the answer is almost always, Yes.

Do you want to make some money?

Randleman laughed. And then said, "Yeah."

"I'm a monster," says Randleman, "and I love this, and this might sound crazy because I don't *like* to hurt people but. . . ." I'll finish the sentence for him: If it happens, it happens.

And so it did—flights and fights in Brazil, a string of victories over the Brazilians, his UFC debut and a bloodline that goes like this: Mark Coleman beat the slop out of a bevy of brawn to take the title; Maurice Smith beat the slop out of him; and Randleman was set to go head-to-head with Smith. Randleman played giantkiller *killer* that day, beating the slop out of Smith and pronouncing, as no empty boast, "I'm afraid of no man." Nice work if you can get it (and he did). But in a just world he'd be starring opposite Van Damme, Schwarzenegger, and Stallone in some Hollywood musclecapade. He'd be training Madonna. He'd be Tae Bo fer chrissakes.

"Our society is so backward," Randleman opines from his home in Columbus, Ohio. "The things that we should embrace and enjoy are the things that we think of as being bad." Like, presumably, the good-ole Georgia head-whippings he's been inflicting on a steady string of opponents, from Maurice Smith to Bas Rutten (whom he lost to in a controversial decision).

"Look," Randleman says, "I'm not in a dangerous sport. Nobody ever left the Octagon in a wheelchair, and the only concussion I've ever gotten was from high school football. But I'll tell you something sad. I met Jack Dempsey's great-grandson, and the man cannot speak. It's terrible. And that's from boxing."

Boxing. The usual suspect. Also under fire in what even Joyce Carol Oates thinks is a conspiracy against masculinity and race, is understood by Randleman as simply being the handmaiden of dueling business interests.

"I don't have the official figures," Randleman offers, "but the UFC at its height was grossing larger sales than things like Wrestlemania and Evander Holyfield–Lennox Lewis fights. All of that UFC money was just making UFC folks rich. It would be well worth spending $2 million on lobbyists to keep the UFC from taking $10 mil out of your pocket, I'd think."

And so it goes. In the seesaw of history, power—that volatile mixture of might and money—resolves itself around its truest measure, cash, while the gladiators soldier on.

"I don't fight to impress. I fight to get paid," concludes Randleman. "And *when* I get paid I take the money and give it to my family and my kids. It's that simple."

And could not be simpler.

MO' TROUBLE, MO' PAIN, MO' SMITH

Back when I sported a konk, I used to have a hairdresser at Mrs. Blue's shop up in New Rochelle, name of Maurice Smith. Nice gentleman, always smelled of Chanel No. 5. Wore angora. But, strangely, I don't think this is him, so I check his vita. Bellevue, Washington, resident, 6'2", 220 pounds, UFC Heavyweight Champion, Extreme Fighting (EFC) Heavyweight Champion, WKA World Heavyweight Muay Thai Champion, ISKA World Heavyweight Kickboxing Champion with 44 KO's in kickboxing alone.

My guess? T'aint the same fella.

And when we speak, I know for sure that we're talking birds of a different feather since words keep coming up in conversation that are remarkably unlike other conversations you might have with a hairdresser. Words like "brutal," "violent," and "deadly." And sentences like "I would never say stomping a guy's head on the ground is a good thing to do." But they come so easily he could just as easily be saying almost anything else, and he homes into that strangely dissonant matter-of-fact.

"Ninety-nine percent of the guys that I've met," Smith's says in his staccato delivery, "and fought with are actually nice guys. Decent guys. Much nicer-seeming than the boxers, who have these violent pasts. And they DO call what we do *submission* fighting, which sort of means to me that the guy at least has an out, before he's permanently damaged. He can quit. Submit. In boxing the way

Kevin Randleman (*left*) and Maurice Smith (*right*).

out is usually when the lights go out. In mixed martial arts it's *not* about killing the guy or whatever, it's about winning the game."

Winning is something Smith would know something about. After picking his way through a variety of martial arts between the ages of thirteen and eighteen (after having been inspired by Bruce Lee's *The Chinese Connection*), the forty-four-year-old Smith began a competitive career that he ended in grand style when he hit the big life marker of forty. That's twenty-two years of stepping into a ring and kicking ass like ass-kicking was going out of style. I mean, I like ass kicking as much as, well, almost as much as Smith, but, I wonder if it's any wonder that the general public can't quite slip behind the veil of why he does what he does.

"They may not understand what it is," Smith says.

What?

"Competition. It all comes down to competition," Smith riffs, "regardless of whether it's ping-pong or volleyball or anything. It's what you're *good* at. What you may be the *best* at. And it's human nature. It's animal nature. To dominate. And we have a choice: to fight or not fight. I want to fight."

So he has, as he worked overtime up to his forty-year-old end date, defeating the previously undefeated grappler and Olympic freestyle wrestler Mark Coleman, stopping heavyweight brawler Tank Abbott and eventually being stopped himself by Coleman protégé Randleman. Smith bristles at the suggestion that this was a classic case of the lion in winter, an older fighter staying in beyond his appointed time, and chalks the loss up to illness.

But then he steps outside of the pro-wrestling volume range by praising Randleman as "a young man of exceptional talent." And there is, if not a warmth in his voice, at least a recognition of a fellow traveler on a road that's clearly less traveled. When asked about the mystery of life beyond the fight, Smith, completely in sync with how his whole career has flowed, doesn't miss a beat. "If I'm not fighting, I'll be training fighters. Teaching younger fighters. Because I love the fight and the competition and there is just no substitution."

THREE
FAR EAST FIGHTING FOR FUN AND PROFIT
(WITH A BREAK-OUT SESSION FOR KNIVES, SHADOWY SKULLDUGGERY, AND MOTHER TERESA)

"There's a point at which the conscious mind just gives up." He sits across from me. Not on the other side of the oak desk but on the same side. Striking distance away. He's about 5'10". Maybe about 185 pounds. You'd never notice him, and that's the key: *you'd never notice him*. His name is Nirmalya Bhowmick, and it probably doesn't mean anything to you. If it does, you already know what's going to be said here, and you're probably shocked he let me say it. If it doesn't, you need to know that this is where we go from sports story to truer-tales-have-never-been-told type of story. Translation: from prototype to archetype, because Bhowmick trades in fighting (dare it be said) for keeps.

The public face? Well, he's the founder of the California University of Protection-Intelligence Management. Former founder of a storied but distinctly and suspiciously non-ambitious academy for the hyperaggressive art of muay thai, the deadly Southeast Asian kickboxing discipline that brings arcing knees and slashing elbows into a picture remarkably bereft of any *defense*.

The private face? That's harder to see, and as we wander the halls of his San Jose, California, based institute of higher learning, all marbled floors, past doors with brass plaques that read *Admissions*, *Registrar*, *Dean of Students*, and well-turned-out white guys who'd be at home in any insurance office, Bhowmick makes intros to the faculty. Business cards are brandished, and the military prefixes affixed to the names start to make things a little clearer. As do the firm grips, steady gazes, and the whole Sgt. Rock schmear. One's just gotten back from Baghdad. Was he serving?

Silence. Then, eventually a slow, sure nod.

Okay. We'll get back to that.

At forty-four years old, Bhowmick looks at least ten years younger. Good clean living, I offer—and this is important—without a single hint of a smirk. He smiles, and in a nondescript back-room office the bookshelf is lined with course study and books that range from *How to Read a Newspaper* to dark-science shit on terrorism, counterterrorism, close-quarter combat, interrogation, insurgency, and protection. The best defense is a good offense, I suddenly remember. But he was mid-stream in explaining to me what his cage was for.

Not the cagefighters kind of cage, the kind with rubber-coated chain-link topped with cushioning foam and turnbucklesque stanchions every few feet. No, this is a steel cage. Like a prison-cell cage. About eight feet across, ten feet high, with an enclosed top and a door opening that is low to the ground. Like they were expecting a dog to be going in there. Or an unconscious man to be pulled out.

"I can tell you exactly when the conscious mind gives up. This is not rocket science," says Bhowmick. "It's usually about two minutes and ten seconds in." And Bhowmick describes a scenario where one man faces two men in the cage. He tells the first man that the other two are going to be hitting him for three minutes. He's to defend and counter. The good part is that they will only be attacking with one strike. The bad news is that they will strike him for the entire three minutes. Whether or not he's defending himself. "The first minute most guys are pretty game. The second minute gets tougher, and then about two minutes and ten seconds in, his conscious thinking just stops and he either starts to use what we've taught him or . . ." He trails off, and then I remember the doggy door.

"The idea is that if you fight from where the conscious mind is, you're just trying to think your way through instead of ACTING your way through it. Instead of doing it." Bhowmick clears his throat. "I want to destroy that whole 'thinking' part of the process and get straight to doing, and the way that you do that, the way that you get to that is by drilling down beyond the conscious mind to where the real learning happens: the subconscious mind. Sometimes you have to do things one hundred times . . . one thousand times . . . through fatigue or stress . . . until that becomes the thing that you automatically do."

But stuntmen routinely ridicule those stuntman schools and those that come from them. Is it possible that although this is the way he's teaching, this is not the way that he learned? Which is to say: We'll do what you say, but what did YOU do? Which is when it comes.

"Well, when I was knife-fighting in the streets of Calcutta . . ."

This is a lead-in that works no matter what kind of party you're going to. No matter where you're going with it.

"When I was knife-fighting in the streets of Calcutta . . ." And he pulls up his sleeve to show a dark cicatrix on his right wrist, where, he claims, knives have come to play. "I knew that unlike the sports competitor who knows if he doesn't win that he just goes home a loser, I was impressed by the fact that I might not go home at all if I was not properly motivated."

And we have to digress upon digression because of the party line that's still got me hooked. Knife-fighting in the streets of Calcutta, indeed.

Bhowmick's family life in Calcutta was as far from the Black Hole as far could be. "I never touched a plate, not to get it to the table nor to clean up after I had eaten. We had servants."

Perhaps the profile of the Calcutta knife-fighter.

"Well, I also used to go to the school, St. James, in Calcutta. It was a Christian school."

Christian Calcutta knife-fighter. Sorry. My correction.

"It was actually across the street from where Mother Teresa had her place. And I used to go over there and help out, and while being there I tried to understand why we had so much while these others had so little. No one could give me any answers that made sense to me . . . but I knew that if I could do something to stop it, or to somehow make it okay, well, I'd be fulfilling a kind of destiny. And this followed me my whole life. So I got into lots of fights just because . . . well, there are two types of people. Those who walk by problems, and the other kind. I was the other kind."

WHILE MY KNIFE GENTLY WEEPS . . .

The occasion was a seminar. The seminar was an invite-only affair. Except the invites were not written, nor mailed, but spoken in a gentle aside, full of the sort of underworld understatement that makes one man mistake an "Okay, now you're dead" for an "Okay."

"I'm going to have a special class. You should come," Nirmalya Bhowmick said in fadeaway, as he busied himself with some stuff behind his desk. I heard it—the strategic use of the word "should." And so there I was later, gathered in a tight knot of others—cops, maybe mercs, er, "military contractors," with no weekend warriorage anywhere to be seen.

(See Walter Salles' classically underrated *A Grande Arte*, 1991, for a filmic, and albeit stylized look into the finer points of what it LOOKS like). The subject at hand: knife fighting. How to, what to use. No mention of the WHY, except it was sort of silently assumed: you had no other choice.

And because you have no other choice, there you are looking at a knife. While any knife can be used for fighting, sort of like any rock you can hold in your hand is a rock you can throw, there are better knives and worse knives to use if you want to use it and live to use it again. Again: if you have NO OTHER choice.

KNIFE: A blade with a nice ricasso—the unsharpened portion of the blade right above the handle—is a good place to start to get a grip on an edged weapon you do not want to lose. A finger twisted around the knife's ricasso (I sported mine all white-taped-

up) slows the movement of the knife out of your hand, or out of position in your hand. If the handle is slightly rubberized (stay away from woods, ceramics, and other things, like stone, or plastic, that slide too easily) all the better. And while silver and stainless-steel handles and blades are good for the movies, with a darker blade and the right kind of light, people might even think you were just dancing, instead of what it is you may really be doing: fighting for your life in a battle you want to see finishing. Keywords: YOU . . . WANT . . . TO . . . be alive to SEE.

Oh, and only use a four-inch blade or shorter if you just want to play. It takes something longer than four inches to get through all the fascia, chest muscles, and rib cage, and into the heart.

STYLE: Filipinos have a kick-ass stick fighting art, *escrima*, which can easily be modified to include knives. Except, according to Bhowmick, "knives are used differently than you use a stick." Because sticks rarely pierce, or at least take too much effort to do so with your garden-variety stick, they stop . . . whereas knives pierce and just keep going. But the mechanics are similar. Let's view the body like an X—two arms in the air, two legs on the ground. IF you want to play, this is all that matters. If you want to bleed someone out sllllloooowwwww. Arm attacks and leg attacks are good. Upward slashing maneuvers with the knife tucked underneath toward your little finger are good when the person you're fighting has no knife (we ain't going to ask).

But if the person you're fighting HAS a knife? Yeah, you wanna go *West Side Story* and hold the knife forward, finger twisted around the ricasso, and think about counting to four, since the fourth button on a button-down shirt is where you need to go to stop a heart. Which is our thoroughly genteel way of saying, ice the motherfucker, whether he's wearing a button-down, a T-shirt, or no shirt at all. Not slashing (play time) but stabbing (work time). There's a big difference. And a lot of times, that has everything to do with what you're going to say when it's over (if you're alive to say anything at all). In short: if you had to kill him, make sure that's a HAD to kill him. Or you're likely to have many more occasions, on the shower-room side of your local penitentiary, to practice your fine new art.

THE WEIRD UPSHOT: Stabbing people is, apparently, a completely wild sensation, as sensations go. "Well, we're all used to our hands obeying certain natural laws when we use them." The speaker, a fellow participant, is neither stocky nor imposing. Much more like a Clint Eastwood. Rangy. And not so willing to be ID'd for quotes like this: "We're used to our hands stopping when they come to a chest, especially fighters, striking-arts guys. But when you stab someone your hand just moves right through them, it feels like. Right on through." And with a wrist flourish he moves his hand toward my sternum, detours around my rib cage, and taps me on the back. "Like magic."

The other kind, who prior to the street scrapping wandered into a restaurant at eight or nine years old and tracked down the Thai cook who he had heard knew muay thai and started on a road that had him at the Muang Surin camp in Bangkok. The road that led to studying with Dentharonee Muang Surin and Sensak Muag Surin (the names probably won't matter to you but know that these are just some more men who could kill you as quickly as they could look at you). The road that had him picking up Pashtun, Urdu, Nepali, Hindi, and English. And probably the selfsame road that rewarded his scholarship in the blood arts with a call from a family friend in the Indian Ministry of Defense, and a subsequent involvement with intelligence work.

And this is where he leans toward me and asks me to turn off the tape recorder and in total life-and-death fashion asks me to be circumspect about what I say from here on out. He could get in trouble. But more importantly, I could get in trouble.

Like the kind of trouble you got into in Burma?

"Oh. You remember that?"

Of course I did. My association with Bhowmick goes back fifteen years, to when he was operating as an occasional gem dealer and full-time muay thai instructor. The gem thing seemed a curious conceit. But what I called a conceit he called a cover, and that, combined with the martial arts, allowed him to travel and train fighters in the art of fighting and other, um, "stuff," you know? And as luck would have it, there he was in Burma. Training students. And that's the way he says it, students. No quotes around that word; in fact, no quotes around almost everything I think should have quotes around it, which is almost everything he's said since he started hinting around the whole "CIA operative" trip. But I must assume that they were real card-carrying students and that we haven't slipped into the intelligence-community rabbit hole where everyone's a "freedom fighter" and words never seem to mean what they say.

"I was training these students and back then there was lots of unrest and one of the students called me one day to say that he had heard that the Burmese secret police were going to pay me a visit because I guess some of my students happened to be Karens. Freedom fighters."

No going back to the hotel to collect his belongings. No passing GO and collecting $200. Just beating it out of Dodge. And, of course, that last-minute twist that makes movies so movie-like: a forgotten, much-needed address book.

"I called back to the hotel and they told me that the address book was there, but that some government agents of some kind had been there, and so I left. Without it. And have actually never been back."

So it goes. Later trips to Dubai. And even more than that. The stuff between the ellipses from the secured server part of the CUPIM website: "Dozens of clandestine intelligence operations, counter-terrorism assignments and high risk protection operations spread over 20 plus countries throughout his career."

Perfect.

The trick was to get those who fought not for fun but for keeps to talk about fighting for keeps without drawing undue and distinctly unhealthy associations with the nature of interpersonal struggle and those who professionally engage in such (and without getting them arrested).

SO YOU'VE BEEN STABBED: SIGNS YOU MAY HAVE LOST A FIGHT

"If a fox is chasing a hare you have two fundamentally different ways of viewing the same event: the fox is thinking very much about dinner. The hare is thinking about his life. And with these come different sets of motivations and methods."

Nirmalya Bhowmick's knife-fighting seminar zeroes in on those differing methods of dealing with edged weapons in a conflict that might see no interfering ref, no timed rounds, and no do-overs. "You must think like the hare. And the number-one thing you must think, as well as say to yourself, if you find yourself in a knife fight, the one thing that might save your life, is your understanding that TODAY YOU WILL BLEED A LITTLE.

"This way you won't be so surprised when it happens." And it seems like, at least on the streets of Calcutta, where Bhowmick cut his teeth, almost literally, it *will* happen. "A knife is just an extension of your hand. Part of your arm. So if someone can touch you in a fight, if they have a knife they can cut you. In fact, I'd rather face a man with a gun than a man with a knife any day. Because a man with a gun might miss. A man with a knife will always cut you.

But you'll do okay if you:

1. Accept that you will bleed.

2. Maintain a mission-oriented commitment.

3. Have a philosophical idealism, or, some would say, faith; and

4. Use aggressive approaches with better technique to win the day.

Dale Carnegie couldn't have said it better.

But even this was a loaded thicket. Lt. Col. David Grossman in his sensitively titled tome *On Killing: The Psychological Cost of Learning to Kill in War and Society* (1996) states that in any given population a certain percentage of pre-existing psychotics will be capable of carrying fighting well beyond the parameters of sport into killing. And do so while suffering nary a negative side effect—hence the psychotic part. This subgroup, less than 5 percent, he rules out of serious consideration, averaged out with the pacifists, before he proceeds with his hand-wringing premise that killing is unnatural.

Bhowmick smiles. "There's a difference between a combat specialist and a psychotic. But if you give me ten men I can turn fifty percent into killers." Useful, I guess, if killer and fighter sit along the same continuum . . . but, in Bhowmick's case it seems, at least so far as he willing to admit, his actions have been protective in nature. For instance, the public face of his university is Michael Corcoran, former Secret Service man, purportedly on presidential detail the day that Reagan got shot. These guys are taking shots, not giving them.

But then I am reminded of the wildly seesawing angle of attack on both of these. After Larry Flynt got shot and paralyzed, security in his Wilshire Boulevard redoubt was *muscular* and structured the way good security is usually structured: present but not too present. Then-executive editor Allan MacDonell was escorting me through the offices, where I was meeting him to discuss my first article for *Hustler*: a potboiler about collections thugs. I asked about Larry's security and MacDonell said significantly, "They do a real good job of protecting Larry from bad things. Sometimes they protect him from bad things before they even happen." And it hung there in the air, just like that—an odd and swinging admixture of ying and yang.

So it goes with Bhowmick's career arc: a Hindu in a Christian school who was attracted to Buddhism, muay thai, the righting of wrongs, the wronging of rights . . . study on the Japanese Red Army, Baader Meinhof, the PLO, and then a sudden superhero-esque desire to stand against the ills.

But when I paraphrase that line from the Nicholas Cage flick *Lord of War*, that every thug with a gun and a dream calls himself a "freedom fighter," he just smiles. "In Darjeeling in the late 1800s there was a monastery, and the monks there believed that life is impermanent, death is unavoidable, and trying to do something good costs a lot."

How much?

He smiles and tells me to come back if I have any further questions, and so I do. I call back several times and he's out of country, and busy, or in the country and busy. I get a hold of him one more time and he's cordial as cordial can be, but when I make a move to ask my follow-up questions he's like quicksilver until I realize that I, in actual fact, already have my answer: a lot.

Times Online
June 26, 2006

CAGE FIGHTER HELD OVER £53 MILLION KENT ROBBERY

By Adam Fresco

A man arrested in Morocco in connection with Britain's biggest cash robbery was today named as martial arts expert Lee Murray.

Mr Murray, who is believed to have been under surveillance for several weeks, was detained in the capital Rabat yesterday on suspicion of kidnap and robbery.

Kent police also revealed that two men had been arrested on Friday in connection with money laundering. They said that a "significant amount" of money had been recovered but refused to confirm reports that it was £1 million.

The money was still being counted and forensically examined today to see if it was connected to the £53 million Securitas raid in Tonbridge, Kent, four months ago.

Moroccan police swooped on the suspect, who is known as Lee "Lightning" Murray, while he was with other men near the Mega Mall in the Souisi district.

Mr Murray, 26, is a well-known cage fighter, who has appeared on television. Cage fighting is a mixture of kick boxing and wrestling in which contestants fight in a cage.

Mr Murray, who is from the South London area, nearly died last year when he was stabbed outside a London nightclub.

Detective Superintendent Paul Gladstone, Kent Police's head of Serious and Major Crime, said that the UK would now be seeking Mr Murray's extradition.

Britain has no formal extradition treaty with Morocco, so would have to make a special, one-off request. The last extradition from Morocco to Britain was in 1995.

Speaking outside Kent Police HQ, Mr Gladstone said: "At 4.30pm yesterday Moroccan police officers arrested a 26-year-old man, Lee Murray, of Sidcup, South London, near the Mega Mall shopping centre in the capital city, Rabat.

"He was arrested for robbery, kidnap and other offences linked to the £53 million Securitas raid in Tonbridge, Kent, in February.

"The arrest was made with the authority of the Crown Prosecution Service, Kent Police and the Moroccan authorities. The man is in custody in Rabat and the United Kingdom is now seeking extradition.

"We are grateful for the help of the Moroccan authorities and Foreign and Commonwealth Office in this matter.

"This latest development is part of our ongoing investigation and our inquiries continue.

"We are aware that some media are reporting that a further £1 million cash has been recovered, linked to the Securitas robbery.

"Working with Surrey and Hampshire Police, we did arrest a number of people in Surrey and Hampshire on Friday and have now charged two men, from Devon and Hampshire, with the offence of money laundering. A significant amount of cash was recovered.

"However, we are not able to confirm the amount at this stage or link the cash to the robbery or any similar crime. The money is now being counted and forensically examined."

Five men and two women have already been charged in connection with the robbery and are due to appear in court next month.

Raiders netted £53,116,760 in the early hours of February 22. Most of the cash is still missing.

(http://www.timesonline.co.uk)

FOUR

JAILHOUSE ROCK

BULLSHIT FIGHT STYLE? OR THE SOUND BASIS FOR PROTECTING YOUR ASS FROM THOSE WHO WOULD BENEFIT FROM ITS AGGRESSIVE EXPLOITATION WHILE LOCKED DOWN?

He rattles off the names like sports teams: Chino, San Quentin, Pelican Bay, Folsom, Soledad. He, being specifically Eddie Williams. Back to him later. Right now I'm more amazed that there's no mention of *Oz* anywhere in there. Possibly because, you see, *Oz* was a TV show about a place where men go to get drilled in the ass for crimes against society. Those others mentioned are NON-fictional, the Ivy League of West Coast penitentiaries, just places where men go to get drilled in the ass for one reason and one reason only: they didn't fight long enough, hard enough, and, ultimately, GOOD enough to keep FROM getting ass-drilled.

But this middle-class preoccupation with man-on-man titillation is about more than underclass class lust, though. It's about a lot more. For men. For women it might be just the joy of a little televised rough trade with well-muscled men doing what well-muscled men do when there are no women around to do it to. But for men, for *modern* men separated from rites and rituals that set off the boyhood years from the horrible sameness of everything that everybody else is doing, unspoken prison fantasies have much more to do with figuring exactly what kind of a man you are. Where exactly you fit on the predator-prey scale of jungle politics. Where with very little else other than your hands balled into fists, and maybe an occasional shank, you will be called on to fight like you mean it.

This is as far from sports fighting as you might ever want to get, and an order of magnitude away from shady CIA operatives fired up into insane action by the good fight. This is the inferno end of the fight spectrum, where losses are measured in a kind of despoiling only dreamed about in . . . well, apparently in middle-class living rooms all over America, judging by *Oz*'s popularity. A prison fight boils down to this: your right and ability to self-define as a man. Or, more specifically, to self-define as a man who doesn't have to bend over when he's told to.

I was being fully mindful of this when I got a call from LA filmmaker Mike Horelick. His biggest claim to fame was a darkly comic and mobbed-up version of *The Crying Game* called *Mob Queen* that starred a lot of the guys who later appeared in *The Sopranos*, as well as . . . you got it . . . The One Time Great White Heavyweight Hope, Gerry Cooney. Mike's question, "Have you ever heard of jailhouse rock?"

And I'm racking my brain and coming up with nothing but *Schoolhouse Rock*, that Saturday-morning ABC television paean to the substandard quality of American public school education.

"No, no, jailhouse rock is this super-secret school of fighting perfected in the nation's prisons. It's supposed to be, no pun intended, killer." Horelick rings off and I'm thinking, "Smells like bullshit to me." I mean, with all the boxers who are ex-cons, how come I've never heard of it? How come Bernard Hopkins in his much-ballyhooed tales of toasting bread with flashlight batteries prison-side never gave a shout-out to the "dreaded and deadly" jailhouse rock?

It is now LATER: Eddie Williams started working in penal in 1979. Wrestling at both 168 and 173 in junior high school, high school, junior college, and at San Jose State, Williams got into the gig during a rough time. Post-Vietnam, pre–post-traumatic-stress-disorder-diagnosis, and a coked-up disco'd-out style of life had him living La Vida Edgy.

"I was stuck in there, working, with some highly volatile cats," says Williams whose presentation has all the lasting earmarks of prison paranoia: standing at your side when he talks, eyes scanning the McDonald's parking lot where we're meeting. "I remember my first time in. People used to want to get busted in San Francisco since San Francisco had the reputation as being lenient. They'd commit a crime in Oakland and drive like crazy to get busted in San Francisco.

"Anyways, I was walking this guy to the cell and I see my boss pacing back and forth behind this counter. He looks up at me as I walk down this hall with this prisoner and he's fucking FUMING. Like I can almost see smoke coming out of his head. I get the prisoner in his cell and when I get back to the desk he starts screaming at me 'WHAT THE FUCK DO YOU THINK YOU'RE DOING, WILLIAMS?!?!? YOU SOME KINDA MAITRE FUCKING D'?!?! STROLLING THROUGH THE PARK WITH THESE PRICK MOTHER-FUCKERS?!?!? LISTEN . . . the very next time you walk somebody down that hall you jack him the fuck up. Let him KNOW he's been SOMEWHERE!!!"

Moving on from here to "Behavior Assault Teams," cell extraction special-ties, and his last gig before going into his present private business of prisoner transport, Williams ended up at the pleasantly, if unofficially named place called The Birdcage in La Honda, California. Residence of Neil Young and Guthrie's Alice's Restaurant. Yeah, incongruities abound. But I put it to him: Jailhouse rock—stunningly effective fighting style or just stunningly effective fiction?

"Well, I've never heard of it insofar as I've been able to observe over twenty-seven years of doing this," and you're reminded that the stocky, not-a-

THE ANATOMY OF A PRISON FIGHT FROM THE NON-BUSINESS END OF THE CELL

A quiet prison is a dangerous prison: "I start my shift and I want to hear the chatter. I want to hear 'Motherfucker this and that.' If I DON'T hear that when I get to work I know to step lightly and lively."

Warm clothes on a warm day: "If I start seeing a guy wearing all of his clothes, I know something's going to jump off. They'll wear everything they own, pack in some newspapers, maybe a phone book. I mean, hand-to-hand in here will much more likely than not involve shanks. If you get stuck, by the time we get shit locked down you could very well bleed out."

Yard fights are different from cell fights: "The space out in the yard offers greater possibilities, and the few times I've seen lots of kicks used it was here. And they'd use the kicks to set up something else. Usually a takedown. But yard fights are a different animal since your time-to-stoppage is much shorter, so it's all about causing as much damage as possible as quickly as possible. I remember this little Latino dude. He was in there for three inside contract hits. He was in there for life, and there had been all of this anticipation before he got there. Well, he shows up and he looked like a gardener. So I wondered what the deal was. Read his file a bit more closely and from the looks of it and as far as I could tell he had hands like lightning. Very fast hands. He had stabbed one guy thirteen times in the yard before anybody knew what had happened. Is that what they're calling 'jailhouse rock'? Probably not. Hard to sell videos of capital crimes."

Well, no, no it's not. But we'll let that slide.

Fight fast: "Five feet across and seven feet deep is a pretty fast ring. What I've seen and, keep in mind if I'm seeing it, and if I'm doing my job, I should be doing something to stop it. But what I've seen has guys moving in with straight punches to back someone up on their heels and then usually into a double-leg take-down that'll end with punches to the loser's face. Repeatedly."

day-over-forty-looking Williams is probably older than you think. "But I can tell you what I've seen."

And people are coming and going in this parking lot, occasionally giving us the stink eye. Years on gang detail and doing undercover work has Williams vibing "con" significantly enough that he still gets stopped and routinely rousted before they find his badge.

"Whyn't you tell us you were a cop?"

"You didn't ask."

And you get the sense that he wouldn't anyway. What is it? Probably the same thing that makes a man want to work with those for whom stabbing is a good career move.

"But you know, I'm probably the wrong person to talk to. The game has changed," he says ruefully. "No one wants to bang anymore. It's all about the poking. So it's not like you really get to see any good fights anymore. And like I said, when I show up, the dancing usually stops. But I got an AB you might want to talk to . . . "

An AB?

"Yeah, you know, a woodpile guy."

And suddenly I feel like "The White Guy" in some street-style stage play where you get all the handshakes wrong and call the wrong people "nigga."

A woodpile guy?

"Yeah. You know, a peckerwood. Aryan Brotherhood." Long way to go for that. "He's about six-five, 230 pounds. Now, HE liked to bang. And if anybody's heard of 'jailhouse rock' it's him."

And he knows you're black?

Williams looks at me, just a flash, a flash that says, yes, you ARE stupid. Because as strange as that might seem to us on the outside—Aryan Brotherhood hanging with black cop—*inside* the walls, where the uneasy alliance between La Mesa, the Black Guerilla Family, the tongs, La Famiglia all hangs together on no sounder principles than any you might find in corporate America ("because it's ALL BUSINESS"), it could just be the most universal organizing principle of all at work here: proximity. Or necessity. Or convenience.

"Yeah. He knows I am black."

And he's all right with ME being black?

"Well I guess you'll find out."

And with that it was over. For him.

Aryan Brotherhood. Jesus H. If I don't get info on the fight game, at least I might very well get a fight out of it.

Yup. Just what I need.

No. Seriously.

OH TOMMY BOY, THE PIPE, THE PIPE IS CALLING

First the phone calls.

The disembodied voices on the phone trying to feel their way around a shape, or form, off in the ether. His? Sort of a semi-non-accented California brogue: equal parts beach boy and thin strains of Okie. This could have been a prison affectation; this could be the popularity of Jeff Foxworthy; but if I'm listening for signs of a raving Aryan ideologue, and I'm not sure I am, I'm not hearing it. I AM listening, fundamentally the way all men listen to other men, for the telltales of their place in space and that unspoken answer to the question we're all always asking, even if we're not admitting it to ourselves, or each other: *Can I take him? Do I* need *to?* The badinage is easy and I'm hearing about his recent gig bodyguarding for traveling strippers and paranoiac Persians with pressing business in Phoenix, San Diego, and Tijuana (hey . . . don't ask, don't tell) until I lay it on the line.

Will he talk about life in the joint?

And you can feel his eyes narrow. Despite his apparent openness, after four years on an eight-year bid for a wide variety of malfeasances, from firearms, to brandishing aforementioned firearms in public, to, finally, drug selling, buying, and possession, he wants to be sure *exactly* what it is that I am asking.

Do you have any interest in discussing this possible red herring of a fight style, jailhouse rock? Or fighting in prison in general?

"Meet me Tuesday at three-thirty. Gold's Gym."

Easy enough.

Gold's Gym 2006 is a far cry from the cinderblock basement gyms of the '70s, which is where it seems like we should meet, all exposed pipe and rusted iron; it's even a far cry from what founder Joe Gold had built down in Venice, contiguous to Muscle Beach and the boardwalk hustler culture. Yeah, it's the House That Pete Built. Pete Grymkowski is the man widely credited with franchising it and turning it into sort of the prototypical fern bar that it is today. But appearances can be deceiving, and as I wend my way between the exercise enthusiasts, squeezing in a fast set of abs, I note that it is 3:28 and that guys who have spent any time at all in the joint seem rarely to be late and so I work my way to the glass doors because I like to be early, if not on time, and I like seeing them before they see me.

And when I do, I make Tommy Kellas right away. Not because he vibes penitentiary, because he doesn't. Well, maybe just a little. But because he's built for it. I mean central casting built for it. To my eye, he's much shorter than the previously claimed 6'5". He's probably about an even 6', but he's also a lot heavier than the claimed 230. Maybe 270 pounds of reddened, bald-headed, tattooed muscle, about thirty-seven years old. As he moves to step past me I try to block his path until we're standing face-to-face.

Tommy?

"Oh, hey, man. How are you?" He holds up his fist for me to touch it with my fist, as his hands are full of gym-bag shit, and so I do. He's got to be the most affable Aryan I have yet to meet. When I ask him where he wants to do the interview—in amongst the potted ferns or outside—he says, "I gotta do some cardio first. I'm 295 now. Down from 345. Gimme about forty minutes."

And so I cool my heels while he stationary-cycles his way to a new, thinner him, and when it's over, we head into the parking lot, where we figure out his junk-strewn pickup truck is probably no place to sit, so we move on over to my ride.

And again: So is jailhouse rock bullshit or what?

"Well, I never heard of it. And I had a few fights when I was in there."

It didn't seem like a man of his considerable weight and strength would have needed to fight, though, unless it was for amusement.

"But I was a Bullet." And then he starts waving his hands through an explanation of his early time inside that's one that you don't usually hear. "And I wasn't 345 when I got there. I was 225 with all of that fucking meth. But I blew up pretty quickly and then I got approached by a guy, um, that they called a 'secretary.' He's usually a guy that's been there a long time. Longer than almost everybody else, and he comes up to you early on and he asks to see your papers. Now, when you're in prison you have all of these papers, papers that talk about your case. I still have mine. And this guy will ask you for it and though he himself is nothing to inspire fear in anybody you need to know that you GOTTA show them your papers because everybody needs to know, and they're going to find out anyway, what you did to get in there.

"So I show him my papers, and then I get what they call 'prospected' by AB."

Aryan Brotherhood, right?

"Right. And you know if you're a white man in prison in Arizona, which is where I was—the Towers, then in Yuma, and then in Douglas—you don't have many choices. It's either AB, the HAs [Hells Angels], the Woods, skinheads or NLR [Nazi Low Riders] . . ."

That sounds like lots of choices to me.
"Well, the skinheads are fucking . . . man, they're boring. They're like Black Muslims. Or Jehovah's Witnesses or something. If you ain't riding with the Angels before getting there, then you ain't getting in. The NLRs are not so big. So it was down to the ABs and the Woods. Which was short for Peckerwoods. Or country boys."

But why'd you choose AB?
"Oh. I didn't."

My intel sucks.
"And I didn't because those guys are serious and it was also pretty clear that at some point if you were running with them, you were going to have to murder somebody. These guys were no fucking joke. Besides which they're getting phased out of major institutions because they've figured out that when you have more than a few of them together the pattern is the same: they start organizing, then they start prospecting, and *then* people start getting killed. So they're breaking them up and spreading them out. But I really just wanted to do my bid and get the fuck out. But even being a Wood, there was a shitload of rules.

"I mean, you see the way I'm moving my hands now? While I'm talking to you? That was a no-no. If I was inside I'd be grabbing on to my pants just to keep my hands from moving. Pretty much everything that other groups did we did not do. We didn't talk loud, we didn't wave our hands when we talked. In fact once we had this kid in there who we started calling Eminem. He had blond dyed hair, the whole bit. Well, once we caught him watching BET, cuz he was into rap and shit and someone said, 'Hey. Tell that motherfucker no go.' And so we did. And he was like 'But I LIKE the music, man.' And we told him no. But he kept doing it so we had to move on him. Put him in the hospital. We just couldn't have it."

So when you say that you're a Bullet, that means . . .
"Well, yeah, after I joined the car I did, the Woods, they just decided that I'd be a Bullet. And my job was to, well my first job was to go to see this guy. Now, the secretary had asked this guy for his papers and instead of showing them, the guy said, 'Oh,' and then came over to me with this 'Are you the head white man in

charge here? Some guy's asking me for my papers!' I told him that I didn't know what the fuck he was talking about but that if somebody wanted to see his papers, maybe he better show them his papers.

"Well, he didn't, and so they sent me and two other guys my size with me . . . and there's something you need to remember about prison. The biggest deal for me while I was there, was the fact that they were only feeding me about 1,600 to 1,800 calories a day. You're a big guy too, so you gotta know that that's going to be tough. So I was irritable a lot of the time. But they sent me and two other guys with me because this guy was himself like 350 pounds, and when we hit his cell we hit his fucking cell.

"He was in the top bunk and we hit him right in his face as he scrambled closer to the wall and we beat him out of that fucking bunk and he was crying and pissing and shitting all over the place. We beat him good."

Did you get a chance to see his papers?
"Damned straight. And we found out what the secretary had just suspected. I mean, what kind of guy doesn't want to show his papers? I mean, what would he be hiding?"

I don't know.
"The fact that his crime was against kids. And he was saying when we were beating him, 'I didn't know how old she was . . . I thought she was eighteen.' Fuck that. Those guys have a hard time in there because if you're in there and you got kids, and you're stuck in there, then you hate these guys. And the guards hate them. And I mean it's kind of fucked up but if a guy is in there for rape and the woman is over age, it's not a big deal. But crimes against kids and you get it from everybody."

Did he fight back?
"Nah."

Are there ways that he could have fought back that would have been effective considering the five-by-seven space you all were in and the fact that there was over half a ton of man and muscle in there?
"Honestly? He had no chance. But generally my sense is that there are a few things that will get you through a jail-cell scrap . . .

1. "If you are a motherfucker with a killer instinct, an instinct to impose your will, and lots of heart, you will do well."

2. "Your basic high school wrestler? I'm putting my money on him. He's got a ninety-seven percent chance of taking care of any situation he is in. He can take all the angles and take away all the striking points, and since what they say is true—most fights end up on the ground—and there's not much room to swing effectively in a cell anyway, I think wrestling is the best." (Tommy is a former high school wrestler.)

3. "Remember that you got to use what you have: sinks, toilets, and the edges of bunks are going to be there anyway. You might as well use them."

4. "Knees. Your legs are some of the strongest muscles in your body, and your knee is one of the hardest points."

"That's the good news.
"The bad news is: nobody fights in prison anymore. In fact, people will think you're a pussy IF you fight."

And this is where they cue the cartoon wah-wah-wah music, because I am baffled.
"Yeah. On a Level 3 yard, which is one of the more serious yards where you can be, if you start fighting with somebody, they'll think you just did it because you're afraid of being in the yard and are trying to use the fight to get out. A fight is nothing."

So what's the hallmark of prison survival machismo if not your willingness to go toe-to-toe, mano-a-mano, with another con?
"It's your grabbing and sticking skills. And if you're an NLR it's your willingness to, and for some reason they go for this . . ." and here Tommy Kellas chuckles a hearty and deep rumble, ". . . but they like taking out eyes. But sticking someone, especially in a Level 3 yard, where you may get shot for doing so, is sort of the ultimate *fuck you* because it shows you don't care if you get shot, teargassed, nothing." And this former nose guard and defensive tackle from Sacramento State actually looks well relieved to be sitting in a car under a tree talking to me about it versus in that yard with "two hundred seventy-five paint-huffing Mexicans ready to shank you.

"I mean, don't get me wrong," though I don't know how I could. "This is a brutal fucking system. Maricopa County. They had us out there in 120-degree heat wearing black-and-white stripes on 1,600 calories a day doing hard manual labor. I'm talking about human rights violations. Check it out on the Internet.

"But you know, when they let me out, they let me out to a halfway house. Which is what they do, the halfway-house thing. And I was in there with Mark Kerr [storied ultimate fighter and subject of the 2003 HBO documentary *The Smashing Machine*]. I had JUST been watching him on TV. I come into the living room and there he is, nodding out from some sort of opiate, and it's a clear violation of my parole to even be in the same house with this shit."

And now with a vision of the semi-schooled prison knuckler versus the well-versed but clearly high, high-level wrestler and ultimate fighter dancing in my head, I ask, laden with expectation: So? What happened?!?!?

"I tried to wake him up to tell him to get that shit out of the house. But I don't know that he ever heard me."

We bullshit now for about thirty minutes more, but my thoughts keep returning to that which I least expected, namely: the clear-cut preference for wrestling as a fighting style that GETS THINGS DONE.

Wrestling?

I expected that about as much as I expected to hear him say macramé or origami. Not that I don't know lots of badass wrestlers, but . . . and here I realize what it is: the juxtaposition of the Calvin Klein underwear models pulled from the Iowa wrestling program versus the *Oz*-based media con. If all media is image projection and all image projection is witchcraft, it'd be less than superstitious of me to *not* assume that the recreational athlete would lose, but there it was. The goddamned undisputed gospel truth. The grappler gets it. Well, we'd see about that.

We shake hands, hands that he had told me had broken not one but two pairs of handcuffs (try it some time), and he moves off, serious as a fucking heart attack.

JAILHOUSE ROCK VS. ROCK & ROLL:
A MYSTERY FIGHT–STYLE FIGHTER DEBUNKS THE DEBUNKERS

"Oh, it's not bullshit at all." The speaker is James Painter, a six-foot-tall, 285-pound Indian. Self-described. No "Native American"isms for Mr. Painter. Washo Indian, northern Nevada, and at this point in time the one voice I've found IN THE GODDAMNED KNOW. And he knows: that there is indeed a specific prison style of fight. Don't know why this seems to matter so much except we imagine that when a man fights, if he is HIGHLY MOTIVATED to win that fight, then the *way* he fights might be something worth knowing. And know it, despite his considerable size and the inherent animal-brain resistance to charging something bigger than you, he does.

"I was in Lompoc Prison on weapons violations. But I learned it from a guy named Skip there. He was in for killing someone in a fight. Skip was Aryan Brotherhood but when they found out he was half-Indian like me, they kicked him out. But he taught me a lot about rock and roll."

Rock and Roll? Jailhouse Rock? Is one bullshit but not the other?
"What's bullshit is this 52 Blocks deal. This is some stuff by guys who have never been in prison. Catching punches in midair and throwing kicks back at them . . . that's bullshit. I never seen that and certainly never seen anything like

James Painter *(back, right)* and his brothers-in-arms. On ice.

that work. But the difference between jailhouse rock and rock and roll is that the BGF [Black Guerilla Family] started jailhouse rock as far as I know. BGF out of California. Rock and roll was an Aryan Brotherhood deal."

And the differences?

"Lots of kicks and elbows in jailhouse. Rock and roll has more power punching or what they call point punching. And limb destruction." And while there's some mulling over exactly how many ways one might destroy a limb, he launches into where talk meets practical application.

"When they moved me from Lompoc, which was a max security prison, to a medium, Sheridan in Oregon, like right after I got there a riot jumped off. These guards had beaten up these Black Muslims and so we were locked down in our units, but not our cells, and so scores were being settled and some of the Black Muslims wanted to take it out on some of the white guys, and so this guy Jeffrey Jefferson, a Blood from LA who was doing life for a drive-by shooting, stepped up and I figured, 'fuck it.' And I stepped up too. Now there are lots of boxers in prison because boxing is the only thing they let you do in prison. Martial arts or any kind of practice of any kind of martial art outside of boxing is as bad as having a shank as far as they're concerned. But knowing this, I just used this thing Skip taught me that we called slap-grab-twist."

Let me guess, it involves slapping, grabbing, and twisting?

There's a silence and I'm reminded that snarky *is not something you probably get a lot of in the joint.*

There is a tense beat wherein the advisability of kicking my ass is probably being considered.

"Yeah. I slap the balls, grab the balls, and twist the balls. Jefferson went down and then I gouged his eyes. At that point this ex–Green Beret named Soldier steps up. He had killed someone for money while in the military and he was a pretty good kickboxer and had training but I caught him with a thumb in the eye and then slap-grab-twist and into a croc roll. Or a crocodile roll. There was a lot of wrestling but I got him and then everything went crazy."

Most would have said that "everything" had indeed gone crazy. Some would have just said it a little earlier. But when I express surprise that the Indians would have sided with the cowboys in this instance he reminds me that, like the guy who taught him, Skip, he's not just half-Indian but he's also half-white.

"Me and Skip met because I had heard he was a tough guy. Things had started off kind of rough for us because I was a tough guy too, and so it seemed like we were going to get into it but it never happened and so I asked him to teach me. We couldn't do this in the open so we went into the card room and held some blankets up and went at it and he schooled me. And I've been training since I was four years old. My father was in the military and so I started learning judo when I was four. I took karate, wing chun, was 39-0 in Golden Gloves, wrestled in high school, took silat . . ."

And the bounds of credulity are finally crossed as Silat, full name Pentjak Silat, is mentioned. The only thing slightly more apocryphal than even jailhouse rock/rock and roll is this Indonesian mystical death art. Cloaked in secrecy, it's like the combat equivalent of "irritable bowel syndrome" or "chronic fatigue syndrome": shit that people say they have, which can be neither confirmed nor denied by any sort of real and measurable empirical test. In silat's case, presumably because all on the losing end of the silat equation are dead. And then you realize that a lot of the guys Painter is talking about ARE in the joint FOR killing people.

So, might it be said that your success inside could be chalked up to your thirty-five or so years of martial arts cross-training?
"Well, I knew that stuff when I fought Skip for the first time," Painter says. "And he still beat me. The slap-grab-twist. How to work the eyes, gouge-wise. Biting. Shoving people against the wall and using vertical surfaces. *I'm* writing a book too, you know? I got my bachelor's in English from UNR [University of Nevada, Reno]. And I got some tapes too . . ."
And now I'm really unsure. Just because people say it is so don't mean that it is so. Guys with pumped credentials, worked histories, grandiose claims are filthy thick in the martial arts scene. Maybe more so than other sporting endeavors. I mean, you might lie about your golf handicap, even an average golfer can pick out a bad swing. But take a man who says he can kill men? How the hell are you going to prove this? This is how karate managed to captivate the minds of America for so long. Its bluster and promise were never put to the test. Mixed martial arts like the UFC, Pride, and some of the smaller ones like King of the Cage, World Extreme Cagefighting, Gladiator's Challenge, and Rumble on the Rock put all of this money where all of these mouths are, and so the most basic question that promises the most conclusive answer: Do any of the guys you train, now that you're out, compete?
"I got four guys [Richard Painter Jr., Raymond Painter Jr., Santigo Terasses, and Dan Alies] who have competed in MMA events. Specifically this

thing up at the Trap Academy in Idaho," Painter says. "They're all undefeated, by the way."

And there it is: what we call fucking proof positive. And we consider the other positives: while it'd be nice to know what he teaches if you got to go to jail, it's probably even nicer to know how to stay out of jail. In any case, it's close-quarters combat, and, outside of a cell, there are lots of close quarters where it might work—the slap-grab-twist, the eye gouge, the bite—but is there really any more to learn about applying those than what you know here? I mean, is there more than one way to gouge an eye? Or bite an ear? Painter teaches the how. But what about the when?

He peppers me with a few more names so I can bullshit-detect if I so choose, and he extends an invite, after I thank him for his time, that vibes right on: "Anytime."

Indeed.

FIVE

THERE'S NOTHING QUITE LIKE BREAKING ANOTHER MAN'S JAW

The place was named Howie's. Seemed very much at odds with the prevailing redneck vibe, the name Howie, that is. Sounded more like a place owned by a fun-loving fella with glasses and a *Star Wars* action-figure set on the coffee table. In any case, that was the name, and it was near Poughkeepsie.

And when anyone around a certain age even thought about Poughkeepsie they'd, if they were film buffs, reference toe-picking and Popeye Doyle. Or at least Gene Hackman as Popeye Doyle as he violated the cinematic civil rights of as many Negroes as possible in the genius non-fight-based flick *The French Connection*.

But to tell it honestly: it wasn't even Poughkeepsie, it was Beacon. Beacon, NY. But "Poughkeepsie" would have been my answer when I was asked, as I inevitably would be: Where was that? Or, more specifically: What was that near?

And it was in Howie's. In Beacon. Before I got put out of the joint by several much larger Marines. This is before I was heavily practiced in the fistic arts. It was before I got put out, but not before I had met Patrick. Up in the midst of prison central, amidst Sing Sing, Fishkill, and a host of other prisons, I was a lifeguard at a kid's camp and had managed to find myself in a position where I was dating the daughter of the warden at Sing Sing (my sincere apologies to all involved in that particular debacle).

Joyce was a comely lass whose father's position in town had made her a hometown heroine of sorts. One night while I was reveling, knee deep, in proud-of-myself mode I noticed the reckless advance of eyeballs of the most impudent nature. These belonged to Patrick. And my animal brain made me do what my animal brain usually makes me do in situations that smell like imminent danger: smile. Warmly. Comfortingly. GENUINELY. Because when you have that faked, much like sincerity, to paraphrase the old Hollywood saw, you have it all.

"You know Joyce?"

Oh yeah. How to manage to say this so it sounded like an apology? Who knows? But the key to avoiding a fight is, to put it most accurately, a process of not necessarily ACQUIESCING, but rather creating a situation where the road to NON-fighting is much more attractive than the road to FIGHTING. Acquiescing invites contempt. The other way, though, the way whereby you meet the threat head on with an embrace that elevates the fight issue to a position of primacy, THIS is the way that signals both who it is that you are and why you are that way: a fighter who, win or lose, likes to fight.

Because, see, then it becomes academic. And difficult: if he beats me, he loses the woman's sympathy. If he loses, he loses her respect. Better, much better, to invert and subvert from within, and this is what I can see in a flash he's chosen to do.

He says something generically unkind about her along the lines of "she's a crazy broad," and I mumble, if not assent, well, then, no ardent defense. And then he starts talking: equal parts threat and entreaty.

"This was the first place I ever broke another man's jaw . . ."

And I was left to wonder if he meant Howie's, the bar stool I was sitting in, or a Tuesday night, or whatever it was.

"You see, if you set out TO break his jaw you might fuck it up fourteen ways to Sunday. Hit his forehead and break a knuckle. Hit his cheek. Anything. But I didn't set out to do that. I set out to kill him. And so, from that point of view, it might seem a pretty good deal for him that all he had broken was a jaw."

He was waving over the barkeep and strangling the bottled necks of Budweiser as he held forth in a general and nonspecific tale of derring-do in an attempt to (maybe) scare me off. It wasn't working. Not because I wasn't afraid, though I wasn't, but because he was being so coherent about it that I was caught. He had applied himself to bar fighting as a science and after about three hours of chatter, and an irked girlfriend wandering around somewhere, he invited me over to the house where he lived with his mother to lift weights and finish what was amounting to his dissertation of the dark art of duking it out with drunks.

His mother's house was a screened-door affair. His mother watched TV and smoked quietly in the lime-green and monkey-shit-brown décor of their living room. We took a sharp turn to the right, then down the basement stairs to his iron shop. It was rudimentary cinder block with York dumbbells and 45-pound plates littered around like so many manhole covers. Patrick was white, about 6'2", and about 210 lean pounds of anger, the source of which was never quite clear, apart from the same sort of malaise that strikes American men of a certain age for certain reasons having to do with the lack of rites of passage, absent fathers, and "bitches."

The story, as he laid it, about the jaw breaking, had as its catalyst some threadbare excuse for "doing the right thing," which I don't think either of us believed. But that's all that's needed in a situation like this: an excuse.

"I hit him right on the corner of his chin. I was going for a knockout shot, and if you look at the point of the chin like a handle, you can swing that head around so fast that the brain just puts itself to sleep to save on the wear and tear. But I guess I swung for the fences because the handle snapped off, which meant in this instance that the part of his jaw in front of my fist moved faster than his head. So rather than knocking him out, I just heard what sounded like a knuckle cracking.

"Down he went, but he wasn't out, see? And when he came up, his mouth was open and he was just going 'uh uh,' because his jaw'd been broken in an open position . . . And he was frantic. No one could understand him. He ran out and someone got him to a hospital. But this was better luck than I could have planned. Since he really couldn't do much more than point, I skipped the whole 'going to jail' thing.

That'll teach him to try to swoop on some chick I'm talking to."

And he did a quick set of bench presses, easily hoisting the 315 pounds we had on the rack up and down for a count of six reps.

"See, these are the things I look for BEFORE I even make up my mind to make my move:

1. Does he have a weapon? A man with a weapon will, without even thinking, keep touching the spot on his body where he expects to find it. If his hand keeps brushing his pants pocket, that's the pocket surprise.

2. Does he have backup? Sometimes it has nothin' to do with whether or not he's a good fighter. If he has a good team behind him, guys who, when they 'break it up,' pull YOU off first, so he can get in a last lick, this can make all the difference in the world. I myself work solo, because most people are assholes.

3. Is he right- or left-handed? You don't think this makes a difference? Then you don't know shit about fighting. I always work the weak side, which, at a bar, is easy to do: stand on the side he's not holding his drink and, um . . . work it.

4. Everything's good for something. Ashtrays, shot glasses, pool cues, and that old standby, beer bottles, are all fair game if you're finding yourself outnumbered or outclassed. I also always consider edges for gaining an edge: the long line of a table, or the bar, or even a back of a chair can be your friend."

But it sounds like you're looking for a fight, and in my personal experience the search always ends up with me having made horribly meaningful tactical errors.
"Well, see, that's the difference between me and you: you're letting your analysis cloud your mind. Sometimes, like with this guy whose jaw I broke, I have a reason, in which case it's a no-brainer. Other times opportunity presents itself, which is always much better than when you TRY to pick an opportunity. I'm just telling you shit that will make you better prepared. I'm NOT saying this shit will work if you keep trying to start shit with guys who are minding their own business.

"I mean the way this works karmically is that those in need of a beating will always find those who need to give one."

Okay. This is getting kinda Yoda-fied for me. Are there are any rules for fight situations to avoid?
"Yeah.

1. If the other guy is too drunk? Well, what's the percentage there, unless he's pissed you off?

2. Domestic disputes? There's no sense to this because inevitably you'll also have to pop the bitch you were just defending, and with that the sympathy of the crowd swings against you.

3. Cops. Enough said.

4. Very, very quiet men. There could clearly be a reason that he's sitting alone. Don't fuck with a dog that's sleeping. He ain't bothering you, no need at all to bother him.

5. Guys who've just come back from their cars with a new sense of confidence. It's usually called a gun."

So that leaves?

"Loudmouths, mostly."

And I did a set and he did a set and the conversation ranged far and wide before coming back to Joyce.

"I was thinking of fucking you up that night."

You mean two days ago?

"Yeah. You were talking loud, hanging out with that chick I liked, and you were drinking, laughing loud . . ."

And you didn't jump. Why?

"Well, you were not afraid, you were more sober than I thought originally, you looked me in the eyes, and then you seemed like a nice guy. I didn't think you were a pussy but I also didn't get any resistance from you. Your attitude was like 'whatever.' Which sort of, in a strange way made me like you."

And then, like suddenly concerned that this made him sound entirely too gay, "But I'd have cracked your fucking skull open in a second if I had to."

I laughed. This was well before I was the 210-, 220-pound fighter in my own right so, of course, I laughed. The meditation on my possible murder while we stood in a place where I could clearly BE murdered very much informed this decision. So we finished our workout and made plans to meet again for subsequent workouts, appointments which I'd keep. But we never drank together again, and last time I heard, he was employed at the local Nabisco factory. The toughest cookie maker in Poughkeepsie.

MOVIE FIGHTS

FIGHTS IN FIGHT MOVIES WHERE BOTH THE FIGHT *AND* THE FIGHT MOVIE SUCK

ROCKY IV (1985): Sure we loved the first one, what with the whole hangdog charm deal and Philly as Mean Streets, but Jesus . . . when Hollywood loses its way it really loses its way. This installment, the most profitable of the whole cavalcade of boxing shame, will cause some to dismiss me as a crank, but this movie sucked . . . even if you like boxing. ESPECIALLY if you like boxing. Curiously enough, with truth resembling fiction and the passage of time, in 2007 this seems almost like a reality show.

LEONARD, PART 6 (1987): We spare no one. Specifically, WE are not going to spare ME, in this instance. Not only did this movie suck and is arguably one of the worst movies made in the history of worst movies, but I was in it. Three weeks of IN IT. With lines and everything, and despite boasting cast members who COULD actually fight (like me) and at least two or three others, this could in no way compensate for the begutted Bill Cosby fighting with ballet dancers dressed as ostriches. A movie that makes you want to strangle orangutans, you love it so much.

GYMKATA (1985): You know who this movie makes us sad for? Dan Tyler Moore. (Related to Mary? Who the fuck knows?) His book *The Terrible Game* was the basis for this movie about a gymnast who combines his ability to dance around in tights with karate to enter what seems to be some sort of early ultimate fighting competition in some sort of unnamed Middle Eastern country. What the hell is it with the '80s and sucky movies?

BOXING HELENA (1993): Not . . . even . . . a movie about boxing. And so, on this count: it fails *miserably*.

DIRTY DANCING (1987): Despite the presence of someone who claims to have some passing familiarity with a martial art (Alex, the correct answer is "Who is Patrick Swayze?") and appeared in *Roadhouse* (also Swayze, in not a bad movie about bouncers), *Dirty Dancing*, despite the premise of dancing in not very clean locales in the Catskills, has a fight scene where Swayze punches out the rich-kid rake but this is no way compensates for the fact that this is a big-time chick flick.

BEST FIGHTS IN
SORTA-KINDA-NON-FIGHTING MOVIES

THE GODFATHER (1972): When Sonny Corleone (real life martial artist James Caan) beats the fuck out of his brother-in-law Carlo Rizzi, up to and including the biting of Carlo's shoe, well THIS scene sums up in total EXACTLY what was going through my mind that night in San Jose of which I will speak no more. That Caan wasn't nominated for an Oscar seems typical for a city and industry that think that there's something daring about Colin Farrell. (Hint: It's called public drunkenness, not daring, where I come from.)

SNATCH (2000): Though director Guy Ritchie's career is caught up in the cinematic chainsaw that is his wife, Madonna, he, at one point, had managed to get his hands around a pretty straight on—despite all of his extant Tarantino-isms—take on underground bare-knuckle boxing. My underground boxer friend Pete was trying to get me a bout in one of these (average take rounded out to about five thousand tax-free American dollars) before he was hounded out of the game by drunkenness and a steadfast refusal to let them professional-wrestlize him into take shorts. Ritchie caught it, and that he managed to do so with Brad Pitt made it all the more amazing. Hey, wait a minute, isn't this a fighting movie? Whatta you? A cop or something?

HAPPY GILMORE (1996): Sure, sure . . . Adam Sandler fights octogenarian Bob Barker. Sure, it was a good fight. But was it worth the $26 mil Sandler got for doing it? Twenty-six friggin' mil. I'd fight *Dr. Ruth* for that kinda money.

SLAPSHOT (1977): The Hanson Brothers putting on the foil. That's all we gotta say about that.

THE QUIET MAN (1952): Victor McLaglen, ACTUAL boxer and wrestler, fought John (real first name, Marion) Wayne, actor, in this flick for like an hour. It was nice to see Wayne get everything that was coming to him, though.

COOL HAND LUKE (1967): George Kennedy has no modern-day equivalent. Neither does Lee Marvin. Or Ernest Borgnine. Or Robert Mitchum. (Does James Gandolfini count?) So when he starts bouncing Paul Newman's head offa the furniture, it makes you cheer. It just makes you cheer.

BORAT: CULTURAL LEARNINGS OF AMERICA FOR MAKE BENEFIT GLORIOUS NATION OF KAZAKHSTAN (2006): Borat, a man, wrestles naked with Azamat, another man, over the latter's lotioned magazine loving of the fur-hating boobie queen Pamela Anderson Lee Rock-Now-Maybe-Lee-Again. A fun-loving flick for everyone from nine to ninety.

BLADE (1998): Wesley Snipes can actually fight. He can so almost actually fight that he and comedian Joe Rogan, who can REALLY fight, were going to meet in the eight-sided ring on the under card at the UFC. Never happened, but if this celebrity shit ever takes off? Yeah, well, I got dibs on Jared Leto.

A BRONX TALE (1993): When Chazz Palminteri locks the bikers in the bar and says, "Now youse *can't* leave" immediately prior to beating them into floor wax. The finest fucking moment in cinema for anyone who ever knew a *cugine*, got his ass kicked by a *cugine*, or knew a *cugine* who kicked someone else's ass.

HOOPER (1978): Burt Reynolds, Brian Keith, and Terry Bradshaw—and Sally Field, just so everyone didn't feel so gay. Great flick about stunt men. And fights galore. Though in our minds Reynolds will never rise higher than he did in *Shamus*, this is a great late '70s dealie, which means? Yeah, you got it: lots and lots of cocaine was killed in the making of this movie.

FIGHT FILMS WHERE THEY AT LEAST FUCKING TRIED

THE BOURNE IDENTITY	GOODFELLAS
TRANSPORTER	ENTER THE DRAGON
RAGING BULL	GLADIATOR
ONG BAK	FAT CITY
FIGHT CLUB	A CLOCKWORK ORANGE

SIX

CURBS, CAR DOORS & YOU

KEVIN WEEKS AND THE ART OF FIGHTING WITHOUT FIGHTING . . . MUCH.

"Sure, sure . . . I get into Vegas late tonight. Call me tomorrow. I'll be glad to talk to you about boxing. And I got lots of Boston boxers who'll talk, too." The speaker was Petey Welch, the *Ultimate Fighter* TV show's boxing coach and longtime Boston habitué, still making his home in Boston—Southie, to be exact. "That the kind of angle you're looking for, yeah?"

"Well, actually I wanted to talk to you about Kevin Weeks."

It was great. Especially if by "great" you mean like what happens when the needle scratches across a record right before the party's over.

"Um, so you want me to talk about Kevin . . . ?" This whole road had been leading up to this whole moment because my contact, also from Boston, hadn't been able to bring himself to tell Petey what I wanted because all of sudden we were all speaking a local dialect far removed from the klieg lights and spokesmodels and celebrities ringside, and one that had everything to do with exactly the ways in which you . . . DO . . . NOT . . . FUCK . . . AROUND.

So it hung there before it had to be spelled out, quickly and more than directly: I had just gotten back from talking to Kevin Weeks myself and he was in no way opposed to us talking about his past as a Golden Gloves boxer, his years boxing afterward, his bouncing in the busing stab-a-Negro-with-an-American-flag-busing-in-Boston of the mid to late '70s, as well as his martial arts competitions and that my interest began and ended there. He paused. "Okay. Call me tomorrow. We can talk then."

And there it was: we had gone from fun and games to not so much fun and not so many games because, you see, in case you didn't know, Kevin Weeks had just (well, February 4, 2005, to be exact) gotten out of the penitentiary, where he had served six years of his debt to humanity. A debt that had been paid as a result of him pleading out from murder in the first degree, extortion, and a bunch of RICO statute shit to the very simple aiding and of murder (and not actually *committing* any of the eight he's on record for) along with an agreement to speak truth to power—or rat on the rats, depending on who you talk to—about Whitey Bulger, crime boss, FBI informant, and now most-wanted-list fugitive from justice. Not fun, not games, but ample and sobering reason for Petey's stall because, you see, Petey still lives in Southie, and really, who needs this kind of action at home?

But screw being at home, *visiting* Southie, you get the sense that this is not the kind of action anyone needs. The place doesn't have the stink of the usual urban necropolis circa mid to late '70s NY with its almost Hollywood backlot blocks and blocks of burned-out buildings and abandoned lots full of garbage. It doesn't seem to draw its power from any sort of public-works theory of ruin. Rather, I notice as I walk down its streets, 6'1½", 230 pounds, as I am the day when I do, and have to step out of the way of a much smaller seventy-two-year-old man who radiated "not giving a fuck" until he saw me with Kevin, its power is one of association. Who you know. Who the FUCK you know. And walking with Weeks it becomes abundantly clear that he IS someone to know.

What I know: what he tells me. From a family of boxers, won the Boys Club boxing championship at six years old, the South Boston Baby Gloves tournament at seven, and before he was sixteen he'd also win the Silver Mittens and fought in the Golden Gloves and the Junior Olympics. Seventy-eight fights *in the ring* and two losses.

Nice.

And despite a family pedigree that included older brothers at Harvard, Kevin took the road less traveled straight into the heart of Boston's whole experience with busing, settling as a security guard in Southie high schools that were fucked to the highest by some integration-mad bureaucrat's disregard for regional politics (pitting the working-class poor against the working-class poor) and then a later move that'd change his life: straight into bouncing. That is, the active application of force in creating an environment ultimately conducive to you drinking yourself into an angry stupor without teetering over into non-drinking assholishness. And for those doing the teetering over: usually a beating.

"Me and some friends of mine went over to this bar," says Kevin. As I am a Brooklyn native, it takes me a bit for my ears to calibrate to his accent, not Boston tweed but something much harder. "And they were looking for bouncers and so we said, 'Yeah, we'll do it.' But they took one look at me and said, 'Bar back.' I didn't weigh so much then. But like my first night there I was hauling ice or something and something breaks out at the door and so I jump over the bar and guys are going this way and that and I fucking crack this guy. Jab, cross, hook, and he's out. After that no more bar back."

No more bar back and on more than one occasion a clear-headed brutality that was noted and noticed by Jimmy "Whitey" Bulger, the reigning head of the Boston Irish "mafia," in quotes here because everything about it bespeaks its complete Irishness: less ornate than the Italian mob, and much more uncontrollable.

And as these things tend to happen, "notice" turned into "worked with" and an association that spanned a lot of bullets, a lot of unmarked graves, and a lot of, um, *force* projection.

"You got to understand something about how we worked. If you didn't fuck up, you didn't see us," said the now-210-pound Weeks. "And if you did see us and you hadn't fucked up you had nothing to worry about."

But what constituted a fuckup? Wearing a belt and suspenders? What?

"It could be anything," Weeks said. "Usually somebody thinking they were tougher than they are."

A common bouncing work–related annoyance that was apparently translatable to organized crime.

But Petey calls back finally: "I gotta talk to Kevin before I can talk to you. You know?"

And I do, and say so, and so he talks to Kevin.

"Okay. Kevin says you're okay. I don't know if you knew this but I grew up in the same projects as Kevin. I fought the same fights. That annual St. Patty's Day show goes back like seventy years. Fathers would bring their sons, you'd train for it for like eight weeks beforehand and if you *weren't* in it, well, you might as well have been wearing a skirt. Or been very good at running."

But by the time Petey had started his climb through the same stops—Baby Gloves, Junior Olympics, Golden Gloves—Kevin was "already the man."

"One of my favorite Kevin stories is of him slapping this kid for something and knocking him out cold with an open-hand shot and then on the way down the kid starts pissing his own pants." Petey and I both laugh, but he goes on to explain, "Nothing gets done that's unjustified, though. He wasn't a bully, because bullies wouldn't last long. Somebody would turn on him. So I'd say he probably never did it without a reason."

And one thing is exceedingly clear in my dealings with the fifty-year-old Weeks and that's that there's a certain clarity to his approach to the world that made sense. Occam's-razor sense. "When I loaned money to someone the first thing I'd ask them is how much they made. I ain't lending four grand to a guy who makes four hundred a week. I know he can't pay. But I'd loan something smaller and nobody ever got hurt if they came and explained to me why they had a problem paying me back that week. But a guy gets . . ."

Chesty?

"Yeah. Well, then, you know . . . I'd have to let him know . . . knock him in the mouth, or something."

And the murders?

"Well, that was Jimmy's thing. They seemed to relax him. I got stuck with the cleanup. I remember once pulling the pickaxe up out of this guy's sternum and his whole abdominal cavity came with it. Now THAT was disgusting. Took three days to get the smell out of my nose after that." And he gives the gas face and leaves me wondering if that kind of clarity, that sangfroid, was natural or just nurtured.

"In the ring, it was all about control. Strategy and so on." We've moved from Kevin's girlfriend's car, a relatively new, gray, conservative-model American something or other, to his spot at Rotary Variety on a block in Southie that he "used to own all the businesses on until the families of the victims wanted to take me to civil court, and so . . .

"But in the ring there were refs, but most of my time in there I was emotionless. I mean, I wasn't ANGRY with the guy I was fighting. In fact I couldn't afford to *be* angry since that meant I wasn't fighting clear-headed. Outside the ring, though, well, anything could happen, and I was prepared for that too. And you know what most people didn't realize: even though I was hanging out at a bar I wasn't DRINKING at the bar. I mean I'd have a drink in my hand but it wouldn't be booze. And I was stone-cold sober. Because I wanted to know what was going on the whole time. Because you never know."

And Petey echoes this, though at thirty-five and successful with his on-camera career it rolls off of his tongue with a certain brio that bespeaks a real joy connected to this chaotic never-knowing. "Nothing beats it, man. Because there's no greater power than being able to walk into the bar, or a club, with your boys, and if a beef breaks out, if someone's mean-mugging you . . . that you could just electrocute guys. I mean, I was 160 pounds when I was seventeen. At 5'11". But knowing that I could lay out a larger guy, have him thinking he's at home taking a bubble bath when he's laying on the floor, well that was great. A coach of mine once said, 'You got guys that want to be known as fighters. And then you got fighters.' Fighting was a tradition in Southie. But that Southie is gone."

Gone. Grabbed by the gentry that's aiming to turn everything into something cute that serves coffee. The old neighborhood character, for better or for ill, is changing. Boxing as a neighborhood mainstay, its underworld taint still sticking, is changing too. "It's a shadow of what it once was," says Petey. "I hate to see it all washed away but this is like the evolution of fight sports. And I'm a boxing guy so I sort of hate to say it but the reality of it is that the mixed martial artists today train a lot harder and are a lot tougher than some of the boxers were." So the race, and the survival thereof, is going to the fittest, the toughest? Maybe.

"I'm much more dangerous now than when I was a kid," says Weeks, hunched down over his Keno card. "I'm fifty. And while I'm not looking for anything other than a job, I'm also not going to take anything from anybody for any reason."

But with the position gone, presumably the money, Jimmy "Whitey" Bulger's weight, and the looming specter of one-way car trips to "We-ain't-seen-him," it seems like it'd be a prime setup for taking everything from everybody.

And Kevin just laughs. "You know they brought Leonardo DiCaprio in to see me. He was doing some research for this movie *The Departed*. So he's hanging out two, maybe two and a half hours, and asking all kinds of questions. Nice kid. And not so short, either. Wide shoulders. But he's asking about everything. Some of it even made it in the movie, but toward the end of the interview he started getting into character and he says some shit like 'When you were an informant . . .' And I lost it. I mean the regular person, well it takes them some time to get from zero to sixty. It usually took LESS than that time for Jimmy [Whitey] to get to six *hundred*. I wasn't as bad as all that, but I was hot. Because I never was an informant. What I told never hurt nobody but me. But the agents who were there were trying to calm me down." He chuckles again. "The kid apologized and said, 'I'll never make THAT mistake again, sir.'

"My point though is that not only do you not unlearn things but some of these things are with you forever, and so when I see these guys on the news, like Andrew Dice Clay or Michael Richards or something, crying and rushing off to rehab and regretting their whole lives, I have to laugh. I regret some things. It's

human. I regret I didn't spend more time with my kids. And my ex-wife. But you'll never see me crying on TV for nothing else I did. Fuck that. I can't change history. That's why you never hear me making a big deal out of only aiding and abetting those murders. If Jimmy had asked me to, I'd have done it. Now, it's not like I didn't learn anything, I did. But I also know that regret doesn't do any good."

Well, what did you learn, say, about fighting? That might help me.

"You know, when we started working on my book [*Brutal: The Untold Story of My Life Inside Whitey Bulger's Irish Mob*] I had some crazy meetings. This one woman suggested that at first I make it a HOW TO guide. Like how to extort people," he exhales, all comedic contempt. "Then I kind of suggested that we should probably just make it a comedy, and she's like 'Yeah yeah,' before I pulled the plug on that. But if you're going to ask me I'll tell you because it's like just what you did when you were a bouncer [almost].

1. Don't drink. In public. I always needed to know what's going on.

2. Jimmy [Whitey] always put himself in the back so he could watch the whole room.

3. When the hitting starts, I'd just always hit with everything I got right out the box. I remember hitting this guy who had like a motorcycle helmet on and I hit him so hard I cracked the helmet. A right cross. I mean I didn't like the idea of having to roll around on the ground with some guy bigger than me. And . . .

4. If I'm about to be done, I'm going out screaming, kicking, fighting, jumping out of windows because at least then you have a chance.

"That's about it."

Almost, or, not nearly. What he doesn't talk about is not even how far could you go, but how far WOULD you go? It dawns on me, that this is the true brand differentiator. If it's not what makes a man start fires, it's probably what makes you afraid of the one who does, and that's his willing and willful ideation of a world where no one fucks with you because you, if called upon to do so, will stop them in the most critical way possible: completely.

And when we drive back across town to where I'm staying, he drives that way. Cars in Boston traffic more like middle-fingered missiles of angry intent, whipping around us, and capably and almost . . . regally, Kevin, not having lost the habits of days being tailed by feds, drives, not breaking any laws, ignoring the beeping and talking about everything at a measured clip until we pull up to the curb. We shake hands. His hands are heavy like the hands of a man larger than his 5'11". There are unasked and unanswered questions regarding who, how, and what's next for him, but it largely seems like these questions are only mine. Which just about says it all.

THE PUNCH LINE & HOW TO GET IT

Robert Mitchum's got his hand splayed out in front of him. The flick is *The Night of the Hunter*, and Mitchum's killer preacher, cloaked in holy cloth and bad intention, explains how the hand that's tattooed LOVE gives, and the one whose knuckles were tattooed HATE, takes away.

"Would you like me to tell you the little story of right-hand/left-hand? The story of good and evil? H-A-T-E! It was with this left hand that old brother Cain struck the blow that laid his brother low. L-O-V-E! You see these fingers, dear hearts? These fingers has veins that run straight to the soul of man. The right hand, friends, the hand of love. Now watch, and I'll show you the story of life. Those fingers, dear hearts, is always a-warring and a-tugging, one agin t'other. Now watch 'em!"

The point is, as he curled his hand into firm fists (and I am reminded here of now-dead comedian Sam Kinison saying he knew what turned Mr. Hand into Mr. Fist), the total import of our species brand-differentiator was driven home: while we can't run for shit (think: man vs. squirrel), our teeth are not worth a damn (think: the Appalachians, the British Isles), the average chimp is three times as strong as the average man (think: Lance Link), and our much-vaunted brains are not worth much more when weighed in the balance against nature's great hunters (think: the common house cat), we can, if given the proper incentives and know-how, beat each other's asses quite thoroughly.

Forthwith the basic punches, and since most people throw whatever punch they throw, incorrectly, here's a thumbnail cheat sheet: a punch is less of a push (ignore Arnold Schwarzenegger's movies as a guide as he throws some of the worst on-screen punches ever) and much more of a throw (think: Nolan Ryan).·

Now knuckle up.

JAB: The lead arm (largely determined by which foot is more forward than the other; if you're right-handed it'll be your left foot, if you're left-handed, or southpaw, it'll be your right foot) extends directly toward the sucker fool enough to still be standing there. This punch should snap and is used usually to set up something else—a cross (*see opposite page, top*), or a kick, or a takedown, if you're a grappler.

CROSS: This is the grandstand of punches. It's the one you usually see in the movies and it's the one in the knockout reel if you're a sports fan. The whole body moves in behind this rear-hand punch as it twists up from the rear leg, with the arm, shoulders, hips, and legs all working to drive the point home in the only way you know how: with a friggin' exclamation point.

HOOK: Like the Captain. This is a relatively wide looping punch that rotates off of the hip and is most often seen at the scene of a knockout as it's *haaaarrddd* to defend against. You bend the elbow while bringing the arm parallel to the ground, and, twisting your abs, swing past the soon-to-be-napping opponent with your fist following. Psychic. Powerful.

UPPERCUT: Remember seeing Mike Tyson, before he joined the lost tribe of ex-boxers, shooting in on another fighter and bringing with him, up the front of his body, and buoyed by the body, a punch that invariably hit the nose or jaw, clicking it shut and with it the fighter whom it belonged to? No? Neither does anyone who got hit with one of these.

BACKFIST: Most effectively and frequently delivered off of a spin (then called the SPINNING BACKFIST), the backfist is a traditional martial arts punch that uses the back of the fist, usually the largest two knuckles, against the temple, nose or eyes.

OVERHAND: UFC Light heavyweight champ Chuck Liddell uses this to great effect more than anybody fighting him would really like. Sort of like the hook but it's all death-from-above time as the fighter delivering it either leans left or right and brings this punch over the top. When Liddell uses it he usually catches them square on the cheek, and though some think it lacks power, not many on the business end of one of Liddell's strikes would concur with that assessment.

HAYMAKER: This is the TV Punch of all punches. And like other shit you see on TV, it's probably most often going to be used by people who learn all of what they know *from* TV. Which is probably the last place in the world that you want to learn about fighting. It's the textbook definition of the wild punch, which finds its variants in other sports as wild pitches and Hail Marys. It is a move that stinks of desperation and, with its windup, a move telegraphed from blocks away, sets the thrower up for any number of vicious counterattacks. The only thing worse than being caught throwing one is being knocked out by one. IF, by some chance, you are knocked out by one, just leave town. Forever. Since that's how long it'll take for nearly everyone to forget that you got taken out by a punch made popular by Captain Kirk.

THE OL' ONE-TWO PUNCH: The first one is the con. It's the slow, stupid punch that gets you to move, dodge, shift your guard, or buy the highly unlikelihood that your opponent is a wash, a bum, a patsy. The Two Punch? That's the one that shows, in no uncertain terms, that you . . . have . . . been . . . PLAYED. Faster, better, stronger, if you don't know this one is ALWAYS coming, then you have no business in this business.

SEVEN

THE REAL SAD AND WEEPY PART OF OUR STORY

I'VE BEEN DISMASTED LIKE CAPTAIN AHAB AND I CAN'T GET UP: A KICKBOXING BEATING NONPAREIL

It was me and Cesar Gracie blue belt (under shooto champ Jake Shields) Sal Russo. Think Hunter S. Thompson and Dr. Gonzo. Except the destination and the journey had nothing to do with Las Vegas and everything to do with Los Angeles and its soulless excess of excess. And we were probably half as high and twice as handsome. At least I was. We were working the twin engines of the good ol' American sex and violence game over at *Playboy* radio's satellite channel, where we were being interviewed by porn star Julie Ashton and some *Penthouse* pet for reasons that are now only hazily apparent to me. We moderated while the porn broads parried questions from truckers about proper etiquette for owning and keeping sex slaves and other late-night lonely-road ephemera.

On the way back, though, sitting blear-eyed in the airport at Burbank, we stared across the aisle at this guy who looked at once totally familiar and completely unknown to us. Like the way it is sometimes with celebrities. Like the time an old girlfriend of mine ran into Brad Pitt and thought she had gone to high school with him. I mean, sometimes that happens. But this time it was the cartilaginous bundle of cauliflowered ears on either side of his head that was the tip off. Sal said it right as I was thinking it.

"Cung Le."

Background: if there was a poster boy for K-1, a kickboxing combat sports group (heavily represented in Vegas and on pay-per-view worldwide) that lets fighters lift from the worlds of karate, tae kwon do, kickboxing, and traditional boxing, Le was it. All high-flying scissor kicks and acrobatic throws, knees and god-knows-what-else from his time as an All-American high school and JC wrestler, Le's specialty is san shou, a combo art that actually ties wrestling in with kickboxing and kung fu. And when I say specialty I mean three bronze medals in amateur san shou world competition with a 13-0 record as a professional, eight of them knockouts.

Let me spell that out for you: his record, including amateur fights, is 36-2, with twenty-six knockouts.

Though his detractors whisper that he's amassed that record on the backs of unworthy opponents, there's no doubt that the 5'10", 182-pound Le can kick a solid yard's worth of ass.

We introduce ourselves and flank him on the matchbook-gray molded airport seats and by conversation's end we've convinced ourselves that we've convinced him to move beyond K-1 and venture into the world of mixed martial arts.

"But I'm going to need some help with the ground game. The submission portion."

And these are the words I've been waiting to hear, as I now offer up my services, on a quid pro quo basis. He'd teach me the finer points of the stand-up game, which, despite my background boxing at the Boys' Club in Brooklyn, seven years of kenpo karate, and a year of the deadly southeast Asian art of muay thai, was possibly a little lacking. While I, in exchange, would throw him all of what I knew about all of the wrestling, Brazilian jiu-jitsu, and catch wrestling I had gotten my hands on.

It was a deal.

A deal that had me making the trek to his fight emporium twice a week. That should have been a tip-off right there, as if I needed more: a man with his OWN fight emporium is probably not to be trifled with. But, to his credit, he did also utter those words that any two men say to each other before they're about to embark on a "casual" run, or a "light" one-on-one, or a "no pressure" pickup game: Yeah, we'll just take it easy.

Take it easy? As if. As if he got to be a world champion by taking it easy. As if I hadn't already put myself, multiple times in fact, in harm's way by challenging the best in the world in some sort of Aguirre-like hallucination connected to delusions of my indestructibility. As if. (This is what we, in the literary field, call "foreshadowing.")

And so it went. My stand-up hadn't suffered as much as I would have thought after a few years of doing nothing but grappling. But it wasn't my stand-up that was the real problem. It was the head trip. The skull game. I mean, the average person, when hit with a sternum-crushing side kick, a kick so solid that the center of your chest burns like a poker was driven through it in some old Hammer vampire flick, would do everything in his power to *avoid* said sternum-crushing kick.

Not me, though. Not me because it was inconceivable to me that he would catch me with it again. Even after he had caught me with it again. Even more so, maybe. You see, my brain was completely incapable of getting it. "It" here being that another man was better than me in *anything*, much less a combat art that had as its *sine qua non* the singular quality of WILL.

And "will" will get you hurt. Because just as hard as he had been kicking me mid-chest to drive off my head-hunting barrages of jabs and crosses, he had also been kicking my lead (left) leg with a roundhouse kick. The standard defense for this in muay thai or kickboxing or san shou is to raise the knee up at the moment the kick is delivered so that it's not delivered full on the flank of the thigh.

But knowing this and doing this are two very, very different things.

And figuring out why you would NOT do it if you KNEW it would save you is something else entirely and probably all goes back to will. Or what my great-grandmother would have called "hard-headedness."

I didn't do it because I used to be able to squat 405 pounds for many, many reps.

I didn't do it because I believed I could take more punishment than he could deliver before I delivered him the punishment that was going to deliver unto me a win.

I didn't do it because, as a Georgian named Time Allen I used to play rugby with once painstakingly explained to me, I was "a goddamned stupid son of a bitch."

I didn't do it for any reasons that might have obscured the mechanical and material functioning of reality, because, you see, what happens to the side of the thigh when it is clear that the owner of that thigh will NOT take the precaution to save it is that the muscle starts to spasm to protect itself. It draws itself up tight. Knots itself in sort of a thickening bulge. Which works at the site of the offense. A site that was getting no rest as Le was Dead-Eye Dick with the kicks, and they came with sickening regularity on that one spot, deviating neither left nor right.

And so the muscle hit spasm, and I refused to have it not spasm by refusing to defend it the way I know I should until one morning when the angry ball of a thigh muscle finally gave way the only place it could: at the tendon. And it was like a sniper had shot me. We had been working around each other in the ring and I had not even been kicked. In fact the first thing he said to me post facto was, "I didn't even TOUCH you." I was just moving, from the right to my left, when I was shot. Or maybe it was more like when a bridge goes, trundled under as a result of the proverbial last straw on the proverbial camel. In any case, I heard it go through the din of blaring hip hop, round buzzers, and the grunt and struggle of life in the squared circle.

I fell to the canvas and, like an animal, I started crawling. I didn't know where or for what reason, and when I finally tried to stand up and put weight on the leg I immediately fell down. And of course, I refused to NOT try to stand up on the leg, and so I stepped and fell, stepped and fell, stepped and fell all the way to my car in the parking lot, where I drove my ass to the hospital and where the lying doctor said it was just a strain and ice and aspirin would help me immeasurably.

Especially if by "immeasurably" he meant not at all.

A subsequent MRI revealed a ruptured quadriceps tendon ("The last guy I saw with an injury like this had been kicked . . . by a horse"), while a subsequent visit to a surgeon and a warning that I was looking at "being crippled for life" if I was going to choose to do without the surgery prompted me to do the surgery. Then six months of rehab after the surgery and the learning to walk again. All pointing me toward the day we all knew was coming.

And when I stepped into that very same ring with the very same Cung Le, I really could not have felt better. He had, in my time away, started training for his first mixed martial arts fight, and as of this writing has fought twice. Fought

SO, CUNG LE, WE MEET AGAIN!

CUNG LE'S FAVORITE KNOCKOUT SHOTS AND HOW TO DELIVER THEM

1. SPINNING HOOK KICK . . . PREFERABLY TO THE HEAD: "I hit one of these in a 1998 fight I had against Ben Harris. He kept circling to my left and I aimed it at his neck, clipped his head instead, and he was out. This kick is generally felt to be a low-percentage move and it's very rare that it works, but I only needed it to work once and it probably worked because of my speed. And to defend against it? Either block it with both hands or just get out of the way."

2. RIGHT HOOK: "I knocked out Arne Soldwedel with this in the seventh round but I switched up on this. I was standing southpaw. And delivered it to his head. And he was out. Simple."

3. RIGHT KICK . . . AGAIN WITH THE HEAD: "It was fifty-two seconds into the first round against Minaro Tauro and I set him up with a jab-cross-hook and then a left kick to the body and finally a right kick to his temple that put him out. I thought it just clipped his head but it did the job. You know, it's funny. If I LOOK for a knockout, I never get it. So I just take what I get and if he's out when it's over? Well, fine."

4. SHIN KICK: "This was a setup straight up. I was punching his [Dan Garrett's] head and then leg kicks to his legs. Either high or low so, that he wasn't thinking at all about his mid-section. And then I threw it all behind a shin kick to his body and I heard two GASPS and that was it."

5. BODY SLAM: "You know, there's this tendency to think that a body slam is just some bullshit professional wrestling move," said Le, shaking his head quickly from side to side. "But you can FINISH someone with one of these. If I'm slamming you on the ground from my height [5'10"], you're going to get hurt. In 1999 I had a fight with Scott Sheeley and slammed him down and he broke his cheekbone. That was it."

6. SPINNING BACK FIST: "I set this up with a hook. When I was fighting Jeff Thornhill I did the hook and just kept coming around with the other first."

7. DOUBLE KICK TO . . . YOU GUESSED IT . . . THE HEAD: "I got Mike Altman in the third round with a double kick to the head. They stood him up after that and what they should have done is stop the fight there because he was done. But they gave him the standing eight count and let him come back out and so while I ultimately put him out with a left hand to the body, he was finished with the kicks. Why didn't I finish him with the kicks? Well, I knew him and he was a competitor and I was just trying to show him some respect."

twice and won twice. Yes, yes. And I'd like to think that I had a little bit to do with that. Almost like someone might like to think that because they *voted* for the president that they've *made* policy. Yes, despite the presence of Hall of Famer Frank Shamrock as an infrequent training partner along with Brazilian jiu-jitsu great Garth Taylor and a host of others, I'd like to think that it was ME. Me and my humble contribution that awakened in him an awareness of the, um, possibilities . . . the possibilities inherent in fucking up some punk whose reach overextended his grasp.

If I am thanked for anything in the future it should be this.

And in the interim, of course, I plan for the rematch that will restore me atop the whale of my destiny again.

I must be high?

Maaaayyybbbeeee.

THE OCCUPATIONAL HAZARDS OF BEING AN OCCUPATIONAL HAZARD

"Yup. It's all fun and games until you find yourself bleeding from a hole I just bit in your cheek." The speaker was, um, me. The occasion was a show being played by my band, Oxbow.

Hunh?

What? Band?!?

Yeah, yeah, Oxbow's been a chicken, or maybe an egg, of sudden and violent action and activity. Like the running of the bulls in Pamplona or some such thing . . .

Or maybe like some wild western where The Kid presents himself as the new boss, Oxbow shows were, on occasion that was almost more than an occasion, beset on all sides by the iniquity of foolish men who—in various fits of *hysteria passio*—felt compelled to, in the heat of a show that touches on suicidal longing, deep sorrow, and a sometimes animal rage, stick their hand into the cage.

And when they did, the response was as predictable as it was rapid: somebody getting hurt (and I'm not talking about feelings. Or me.) and art and the creation of it being defended by non-standard bearers of Eros who righteously embraced the hard truth that whether the rock hits the glass or the glass hits the rock, it's probably not going to work out so well for the glass.

So while my injury at the hands of Cung Le, or rather the flung feet of Cung Le, was as predictable as getting burned when you're playing with fire (and most ring fights are; predictable, that is), it's the exact opposite trade when plied in the streets. Or on the stage. Or anywhere where the amateurs are pressed into believing it's "their night." The injuries are eccentric and frequently horrific examples of what happens when good fortune runs out and bad fortune rushes in.

Don't believe me? Fine. My infrequent instances in such-like street involvement could be only anecdotal or hyped hyperbole. Not so for our resident medical authority on all things related to ass and its kicking: Dr. Steven G. Ballinger, M.D., who knows nothing if not his way around a goddamned emergency room.

Is there any sort of pattern to the fight injuries you're seeing?

"Most of the really awful fight injuries I have seen are the result of one of three things: A freak punch, a lopsided donnybrook, or an unexpected act of God superimposed on boys being boys.

"For example, the most remarkable freak punch injury I saw was a guy who smarted off to a skinny wimp in a bar in front of the wimp's girlfriend. The wimp roundhoused the guy, who wasn't expecting it, and he went down.

"Dead.

"From a single punch from a 150-pound pencil-armed weenie. The punch was just right: full force, directed through a bony fist into the guy's upper lip, and straight on. Two of the guy's dural arteries tore off and his brain was getting pushed out the hole in the base of his skull by the time he hit the floor. Witnesses said that the dead guy didn't even make a sound, except when he went 'whump' on the floor."

Oh big friggin' deal. That sounds like Friday night at my house. What else you got?

"There was another time when a guy came in who had been head-butted in the side and his lung was punctured. He had four broken ribs, a chest full of blood, and his right lung and all the blood were pushing his heart into his other lung, collapsing it. The guy with the bum lung was about 6'7", the guy who head-butted him was about 5'2", but pretty wiry. We stuck a chest tube in the right side and sucked out all the blood, his lungs blew back up and he did all right.

"But in the lopsided category a lot of the really ugly stuff comes from a guy being down on the ground with three or four guys kicking him. My dad always told me never to kick anyone on the ground unless you intended to kill him, and there is a lot to that. . . .

"One guy came in who was still alive, but his head had been kicked so much that it was hard to tell where his face was. He had a shaved head, but the skin had been degloved from his face and head and his lips and jaw were all pulverized. His nose was just a couple of round holes. One ear was gone and the other looked like an old rag. Amazingly, he was awake and trying to talk, but his tongue was just writhing around in a wet bloody hole, with spit and blood dribbling out.

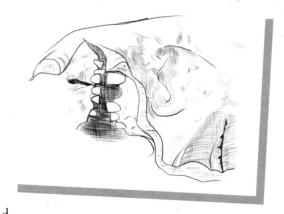

"We wired his jaw and sewed everything back up. His eyeballs weren't ruptured, and when I saw him a few weeks later he looked fairly humanoid. He had a picture of what he looked like before the beating that he brought to help the doctor, and he was an ugly fucker anyway. 'You can't make chicken salad out of chicken shit,' he said. I always wondered why those guys were so pissed at him."

Okay. Now there is a possibility that I am completely nauseated.

"Oh no. WAIT . . . In the act-of-God category one really stands out—he was a rapper in the 'Biggie' mold who was bustin' a few rhymes at the expense of some thug in the audience. The thug met him in the parking lot and proceeded to rap with his fists. The victim tried to run away, and stepped off a five-foot wall into a hole. His ankle dislocated, the bone broke, and his ankle bone tore through his skin. He was so big that he didn't stop falling until he hit the bottom of the mud-and-God-knows-what hole, and when I met him his foot was up halfway to his knee, sticking out like a flipper, and there was about eight inches of bare bone hanging out of the wound. The end of his bone, with the joint cartilage on it, had a bottle cap embedded in it. He patched up nice, and went on to rap again."

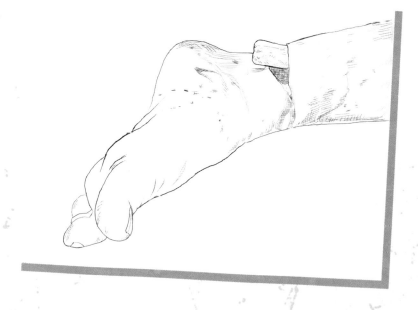

And the world thanks you, I'm sure.

"I got two more for you, though. This kid challenged a classmate to a kung-fu battle for stealing his twelve-sided die or something. He showed up to the fight with nunchucks, but his opponent said, 'No way, dude, fists only.' The kid set his chucks down and proceeded to enter the dragon. At some point his opponent kicked him and he fell back on the nunchucks. One of the handles got stuck right into his side and tented out his stomach right under the ribs. The paramedics brought him in with a bandage wrapped around him, the nunchuck handle strapped to his chest. The fight was over, and the kid lost a few feet of intestine.

"Which leads me to the worst one of all. Some kids in the back of a pickup truck were driving around, throwing stuff at adult pedestrians and generally deporting themselves like juvenile delinquents. One of the kids yelled something at a forty-ish Asian man, and threw a bottle at him. The Asian man shouted something back, and the kid, obviously hopped up on something, jumped out of the truck and rushed the guy, yelling 'What are you gonna do about it Chinkee?!?' or something to that effect. The Asian guy pulled out a snubnose .357 and shot the kid right in the eye. There was hole bigger than my fist in the back of the kid's head. The guy was a Cambodian gangster. The wrong guy to mess with, apparently."

Apparently.

EIGHT

THE ONLY FIGHT SPORT MENTIONED IN THE BIBLE

THE VERSES IGNORED BY PLACARD-WAVING PRICKS

AT FOOTBALL GAMES: GENESIS 32:25

20 . . . Behold, thy servant Jacob is behind us. For he said, I will appease him with the present that goeth before me, and afterward I will see his face; peradventure he will accept of me. . . .

24 And Jacob was left alone; and there wrestled a man with him until the breaking of the day.

25 And when he saw that he prevailed not against him, he touched the hollow of his thigh; and the hollow of Jacob's thigh was out of joint, as he wrestled with him.

26 And he said, Let me go, for the day breaketh. And he said, I will not let thee go, except thou bless me.

27 And he said unto him, What is thy name? And he said, Jacob.

28 And he said, Thy name shall be called no more Jacob, but Israel: for as a prince hast thou power with God and with men, and hast prevailed.

29 And Jacob asked him, and said, Tell me, I pray thee, thy name. And he said, Wherefore is it that thou dost ask after my name? And he blessed him there.

30 And Jacob called the name of the place Peniel: for I have seen God face to face, and my life is preserved.

31 And as he passed over Penuel the sun rose upon him, and he halted upon his thigh.

32 Therefore the children of Israel eat not of the sinew which shrank, which is upon the hollow of the thigh, unto this day: because he touched the hollow of Jacob's thigh in the sinew that shrank.

Translation: Though this might sound like a weekend in Key West to the untrained eye, the subtext for thems that have got the eyes to see is this: um . . . er, well I'm not the world's best or biggest biblical scholar. Maybe it means that the fight style of choice of quasi-divine beings of shadow and light (as well as ancient Greeks . . . wrestling is also mentioned in the *Iliad* and the *Odyssey* . . . and American politics too, I mean Honest Abe Lincoln was a wrestler's cognomen if I ever heard one) is . . . yup, you got it: wrasslin'.

GRAPPLE THIS!

As the old saw—as popularized by the first family of grappling arts, the Brazilian Gracies—goes, most fights end up on the ground. Or as the widely proclaimed God of Professional Wrestling (when professional wrestling wasn't mere muscle ballet) Karl Gotch said, "Bulls die on the floor." So it is that if you're going to scrap, the progression will go thusly:

1. You and your opponent will begin punching each other on or about the facial area.

2. The one who draws the greater number of punches to the facial area, or who, as it is established, will not be able to return the punches, hereupon begins to . . .

3. Grab their opponent to either staunch the flow of punches to the grill or to work on a Plan B that involves, if they're lucky, a knowledge base that will have them immobilizing the opponent through the careful application of chokes, armbars, and leglocks that hyperextend the joints of the arms and legs.

4. When one of these are successfully locked in, the loser will begin mewling like a small child and the fight is officially declared over, with great ridicule to be heaped upon the soon-to-be-departing Loser.

This is grappling.

To the untrained eye? A lot of apparently man-on-man closeness (those suffering from homosexual panic need not apply). To those in the know, or in the grips of those in the know: extreme pain delivered expertly.

Herewith, the basic terms and nomenclature of the laying on of hands.

GRAPPLING HOOKS

ARMLOCKS/ARMBARS [also known as the *kimura*, the key lock, *wakigatame*]: The fighter takes the opponent's arm and by applying pressure to the elbow joint cranks the arm, or shoulder, in a direction that carries it beyond the failure point. In some cases the fighter lies on top of the opponent's torso at a 90-degree angle. Grabbing the opponent's wrist with his near hand so that the opponent's hand is palm-to-the-sky and fully bent and held down. Reaching under the opponent's arm with his other arm and grabbing hold of his other arm's wrist, he forces the soon-to-be loser's elbow upward. This is a true submission hold. Translation: if you don't "*no mas*" on this one, you will lose the arm. Plain and simple.

CHOKES [triangle chokes, sleeper holds, *mata leao*, rear naked chokes, guillotine chokes]: Arms can be confusing. If you look at your arm, it is tri-segmented. At the wrist, at the elbow, and at the shoulder. And you have TWO of them. Unless you drum for Def Lepperd. But the NECK? Well, there's just one of those. And it's easy to find. You see, it sits right under the mouth that's calling you out. Paradoxically, the neck can be grabbed and attacked a number of different ways.

Sleeper Hold: A sleeper hold is generally applied in the following manner: the person applying the hold positions himself behind his opponent. The person then wraps his right arm around the opponent's neck, pressing the biceps against one side of the neck and the inner bone of the forearm against the other side. The neck is squeezed inside the arm extremely tightly. Additional pressure can be applied by grabbing the left shoulder with the right hand, or by grabbing the biceps of the left arm near the elbow, then using the left hand to push the opponent's head toward the crook of the right elbow. At this point (or during the process) the opponent should be brought to the ground if he's not already there. This helps to avoid various self-defense techniques designed to protect against assault from the rear, such as instep stomps, shin stomps, and groin strikes. The opponent will typically go limp after 5-10 seconds of very hard pressure, at which point it is preferable to immediately release pressure, so as to not cause death. Or brain damage from both loss of oxygen *and* blood to the brain. Rear naked chokes, *mata leao* (or, lion-killer) chokes are all essentially the same thing.

Guillotine Choke: In a fight with three-time US Greco-Roman national champ, UFC scrapper and International Cage Fighting king Darrell Gholar I got GOT with this three times in a row. In my first bow in an underground submission-fighting tournament, I got caught with this once, first time out. Easy to avoid, not so easy to withstand, the guillotine is what happens when a fighter applies a front sleeper hold and takes the other fighter downward, while cinching hands underneath the neck, pulling up and holding the back of the neck either against the body or under the armpit.

Triangle Choke: One fighter will, using a poorly placed opponent's head and arm, wrap his legs around the loser's neck. One leg goes around and behind the neck while the other leg crosses over the top of the first leg's ankle. It's at this point that the person applying the choke begins cranking their legs tightly down. If their opponent is unschooled, the natural reaction is to pull out. This only makes it worse as it exposes the neck to more choking. It should be noted that for extra credit the applicant of said choke can, with their free hands, punch the living crap out of the soon-to-be sleeper. If you're fighting someone with a triangle tattoo? You might reasonably expect this choke to be somewhere in the mix.

Facelock: You face your opponent, who is bent forward, like maybe you just went for the guillotine and missed. You adapt and instead press the forearm bone that runs along the line of the thumb against the cheekbone, the eye socket, the face. You then grab the arm with your free hand to lock in the hold and compress your screaming opponent's face.

LEG LOCKS: A lot like the arms, the legs are tri-segmented with break points at the ankles, knees, and hips. Added benefit? Most people can't fucking dance—you think they're going to be able to keep their legs away from you? Noooo. . . . so, if you can't even remember but one leg lock, or hold, you'll be infinitely better off knowing than you will not knowing what to do when the other guy's lower leg finds its way into your hands, either as a result of an errant and poorly thrown kick, or because you've swept in and grabbed it: lift the grabbed lower leg from the base of the foot to the shin and wrap both arms around the foot, placing one arm around (and underneath) the ankle tightly and resting on the foot where the toes are with the weight of your body while pulling up with the bony part of your forearm against their Achilles tendon. A variation of this move is the grapevine ankle lock, in which you fall to the mat and scissor the leg of the opponent. This stops the opponent from rolling out of the move and makes it harder for him/her to crawl to the ropes but lessens the pressure that can be applied.

SUB-GENUS: TAKEDOWN: Though technically not a finishing hold, or a submission maneuver, a good takedown has been known to end the best of fights in the crudest of manners: a head that hits a floor and knocks out an opponent is as good as a fist that does the same. At the very best this is what you have; at the very worst you've just set up one of the above locks or chokes. And there are many, many takedowns with many, many names that may or not make sense to you—high crotch, under arm spin, fireman's carry, inside trip, suplex (not something you live in but a throw)—but we'll go over the basics:

DOUBLE LEG: There's not a lot of mystery to the mysteries of the world's oldest sport. Lunging in the way you might imagine a fencer to do, you come underneath your opponent, grab behind his legs, and lift them up and off to the side, edged one way or another by your head, which is close ranged against his body. When you're in this close it's hard to be punched or kicked here, and with the exception of an opportunistic guillotine choke that you may have opened yourself up for by sticking your neck out, this move is a good, all-purpose Captain Kirk–esque move: deceptively simple-looking but devastating when applied correctly. The counter to this is called a sprawl, which looks remarkably like the end position on those horrible squat thrusts that every single gym teacher in America made you do.

SINGLE LEG: Very much the same but involving, true to its name, only a single one of your opponent's legs. Benefits are that it is easier to get and hold in the face of a good sprawl. Drawbacks are that leaving one leg free leaves one leg that could kick the crap out of you. But our advice? If you have a single leg? YANK it. They'll go down.

GOTCH, LEBELL, GABLE: THE HOLY TROIKA OF TRUE TOUGH

Karl Gotch

I had heard this story from Lou Thesz once. And because I don't want to waste my energy throwing you a beating when you ask me, as you're more than likely to, "Who's Lou Thesz?" I'll just tell you that Thesz was a six-time world heavyweight champion back when professional wrestling was a bit more than professional acting. Thesz said that at one point his fellow German-Hungarian wrestler Karl Gotch had been training this kid and as part of his training he had thrown rice on the mat where the kid was kneeling. After about an hour of this dance of a thousand deaths, the kid had asked for a drink of water, and purportedly a sympathetic Gotch had said, "Are you thirsty, kid? I'll get you some water." And he trundles off and comes back with a rusty groin cup full of brackish water, which he extends to the kid while cackling evilly.

"What? Thesz said that? No. HE was the sadist, not me," insists Gotch, now based in Tampa, Florida. "My grandfather had always told me to treat others the way I wanted to be treated." Which, of course, causes *me* to chuckle, since the school that Gotch, the last living link to a wrestling style that casually has *hooks*, *rips*, and *stretches* as part of its repertoire, hails from is distinctly the purview of guys who only knew one way to play it: hard. Real hard. So despite him doth protesting too much, I *know* what it's like to roll with one of these old cats as I was actually stupid enough to get on the mat with Thesz (RIP, April 28, 2002) in 1998 or thereabouts. That would have made him about eighty-two years old at the time, and the sensation almost can't be described in terms not usually reserved for anything other than natural disasters.

You ever been in an earthquake? Tidal wave? Riot?

Well, that's what it felt like: all impending doom, and then sudden and rushing horror, and then, finally, pain. You might be laughing now, but it was clearly no fucking laughing matter. And the idea that another person, a person who KNEW exactly how the body worked, could do this, was the stuff that lasting nightmares are made of.

So when Gotch goes all peaceful warrior on me, I'm not believing it for a second. Now, I'm not saying these guys are not nice guys (I'm not saying this for about five reasons, all of them good, and all of them having to do with, say, my arms, legs, and neck), I'm just saying that Gotch is a different kind of a cat. He, and even Lebell, is to the manner born. Both were hustled off by mothers in response to their youthful intransigence and involvement in street fights and virtually deposited in the care of—well, in the case of Lebell, Ed "Strangler" Lewis, and in Gotch's case, a Belgian tavern that was home of the United Strength Testers, a loose collection of wrestlers, grapplers, and tough guys.

"They trained three times a week. Tuesday, Thursday, and Sunday mornings. Seven p.m. during the week, eleven a.m. on Sundays," says the still-steely-at-eighty-two Gotch. "I started with boxing and wrestling. My father was a sailor and thought this would be good for me, but my mother screamed murder when she found out. I was not too good-looking already," he laughed, "so it was just wrestling for me."

The older guys—keep in mind it was a tavern—had decided to haze the big-for-his-age Gotch and administered beating after beating to the ten-year-old just to see if he'd stay. "I told them to do their best because I was not going to stop coming. And believe me, it all goes into the bank [the beatings], where it gathers interest, and one day I'm going to be glad to pay you back."

Did he?

"Well, I would have . . ." World War II bites though and in 1940 he was gone. "They just picked you up off the street and carried you away. I was on a train from Antwerp to Hamburg. Hours on a train. And when I got to Hamburg they made me work on the trains. I was a fireman, which meant, then, shoveling coal into the engine. The work was okay but I was always hungry and I couldn't sleep."

Nightmares?

"Russians. They'd play music all night and sing. I eventually got a job repairing the trains with some French prisoners of war. There was one sonuvabitch from Marseilles there who thought I was German. I mean I had learned German and my mother was German, but Flemish was my language. We got into it, and I worked him over, tossed him in this ditch. You know, sometimes it pays to be handy with your fists."

And from there, after they let him go to back home in 1943 for more work that'd make a man out of any mack: blacksmithing. "People complain about what's going on in Iraq now, but in Belgium then, the Americans, our *allies*, were dropping bombs all over. Like Easter eggs. So it was tough. People were dying all over the place." And from this idyll to the final crucible chapter: hauled off to a concentration camp in Kahla, in Germany, then to a factory where they made the buzzbombs. Rescued, finally, by the Russians (and Americans), Gotch settled into a post-WWII occupation of ease: MORE blacksmithing.

"But then I went to the European Championships in 1946 in Stockholm," says Gotch right before he zigs when I expect a zag. "Where I got my ass handed to me." It was his sand-in-the-face moment, and two years later, at the Olympics, at age twenty-four, he was taken the long way around by the gold-medaling Turk. "He was good but I had gotten better enough to not be beaten outright. My neck was raw from bridging. But this Turk came up to me after the match was over and said that I was very good. I told him 'Yeah. But you still beat my ass.'" At this remove of years and more accolades than many of us will ever accrue for almost anything, you can see he still feels the sting keenly. "Of course, the Turk's now dead." So, if not a victory in the ring, well, in the long race, then.

And then change: "I didn't want to go pro because I was in love with amateur. I wanted to get my revenge in the amateur, but at this point I had a wife and a kid and I figured out that I could make in seventeen minutes what it took me two weeks to make swinging a sledgehammer. So I started doing pro matches and then someone casually told me about these fellows up in Wigan, run by Billy Riley, and said I should stay away from them because they would tear me a new asshole. Well, I needed a new asshole, so off I went.

"I go in there and it was nothing like people make it seem. People who never have been there. It was a wood floor, stone walls, and a tin roof. And these guys in there were like a pack of hungry wolves. So I pick the biggest guy in there and I take him down like I would in amateur wrestling, and once we're down he grabs my ankle, and I'm screaming, 'What the hell are you doing?' And he says, 'Wrestling.' So I say, 'Oh. That's how you wrestle, eh?' and we go again and I head-butt him and try to run him into the wall. So, yeah, this is where I picked up what they now call 'Lancashire catch' [a catch-as-catch-can fight style]."

This style was heavy on what are now called submission holds. There were just more of them and they were way more severe. Wrists, elbows, shoulders, and their southland peers, ankles, knees, and hips, were routinely torn. You might get better if you stayed, but if you stayed you'd probably never get well. "Riley abused all his boys," Gotch says. "I called his place the Snakepit, and it was Riley's place, no doubt. He was a promoter and he did like promoters have always done, almost destroyed the sport they're promoting. First they get rid of the tough guys who won't take falls for nobody. Then they get rid of the athletes who even though they take the falls well they still got their pride. Now they're only left with actors who act like they can fight. I mean, you don't believe me? Look who made it great. Look who it took to make it great: the Americans. All of these immigrants, all of these nationalities, and so I came too. Got to Chicago and met up with Thesz, and he was a tough sonuvabitch. But I wiped out three guys when I got there and nobody wanted a piece of me. It was 1959. Finally Big Bill Miller took me to Japan, and Japan saved me. I could make $500 a week there. Big money then.

"But they were disappointed when they saw me. They were used to sumo then, and they said, 'He's so small.' I was 6'1" and over 220 pounds. Well, Jim Wright told the Japanese that he would work for three months for free if I didn't go through all of their guys in an hour. And so I did."

Of course he did.

And so it went, year after year, he crushed them all. All. Of. Them. He's revered in Japan today by those very much in the know as the God of Pro Wrestling. And by this no one means the fake shit, but the very real *professional* thing. Living today, alone, with the exception of a stray cat he feeds on occasion and a loose confederation of guys like Gene Lebell and other known associates, Gotch fends off looky-loos, fight geeks, and professional hucksters with a mixture of bluster and real serious hostility ("Ultimate fighting? I call it ultimate shit") because his love and affection for what he calls the best sport in the world is almost messianic and it seems like he's the last messiah. "It's like Archimedes said, 'Give me a lever and I can move the world.' But he didn't tell you where to put the goddamned fulcrum. THAT'S wrestling. It's leverage, it's mathematics, it makes you think and it prepares you for life. You don't have to be big even. I fought some blind guy in Nebraska and I went out there feeling sorry for him until he got his hands on me and gave me good as I've gotten from anybody who can see.

"But this country . . . I've met more assholes here than I have anywhere else in the world because they don't know what they have. But I'll tell you what they don't have anymore: PROFESSIONALS. And people who can teach it the way it should be taught. Good coaches. And this will kill it stone dead."

He gets quiet and I think of that line from *Apocalypse Now*. It was Dennis Hopper's, "When it dies . . . when HE dies . . ." He's talking about Kurtz, and I'm talking about Gotch and something like the soul of the last great democratic, meritocratic sport around. Or maybe I'm just talking about what happens when tough guys go away and are not replaced with anything other than metrosexuality and talk shows. What happens then? I guess we'll find out . . . all in due time.

KARL GOTCH'S GUIDE TO GREATNESS: A PRIMER

1. You need five things to be a great fighter: technique, agility, speed, endurance, and reflexes. Strength means nothing.

2. You want to get stronger, though? Stop lifting weights. Start using the still rings.

3. No matter how fancy a car is, if it runs out of gas, it's done. I am a fanatic for conditioning. And not the kind boxers get from road work. That's great for boxers because it is how they fight. On their feet. It's good for the footwork. But wrestlers need something else. They need to work the road: dog waddles, leapfrogs, fireman's carry if you have someone else to train with. Visualize yourself with your opponent and go through the moves while you're running. It will look strange but what the hell do you care?

Judo Gene LeBell

"He gets all these people like Jesus, Moses, Muhammad, Buddha . . . all the notables in the history of religion and they have wrestling matches to see who is going to rule the world for the next thousand years. They're all going at it and I come out of the sky and I'm L. Ron Hubbard. He had red hair like I have. So I pin all these guys and then I say, "Who is your messiah now?"

Gene LeBell—JUDO Gene LeBell—vibes a generous self-satisfaction. A generous and contagious self-satisfaction and the kind that probably comes from being extremely good at something (anything) that you love. He's talking about a bow he recently took on *The Mind of Mencia*, a Comedy Central sketch-comedy deal, but he might as well be talking about that which has marked his entire seventy-four-year tenure on this planet: a willful desire to conquer and control while having fun doing both (or maybe it's the other way around and there is no enjoyment without the conquering and the controlling).

Introduced to wrestling by the only woman inducted into the Boxing Hall of Fame, the famed owner/operator of LA's Olympic Auditorium, Aileen Eaton (also known as his mother), LeBell, well before he found his way to Gotch and Thesz, was learning as a seven-year-old at the meathook hands of Ed "The Strangler" Lewis. That'd be THE Ed "The Strangler" Lewis (like you expect someone named The Strangler to suck).

"So Ed says to me, 'What do you want to learn?' And I didn't know. I mean, I was seven years old. So I saw some rough tough guy with cauliflowered ears and said, 'I wanna learn how to get my ears like that. That's what I want.' And Lewis told me, 'Those come from LOSING. Not from winning.' And so he laid it down: 'You got Greco-Roman, which is from the waist up; freestyle, which is from the waist up and the waist down; kicking; boxing; and grappling.' Well, I had never heard of this grappling before and so I asked him what it was, and he said that it was a combination of everything, and so I was sold."

Sold enough so that over the last bunches of decades LeBell's either coached or fought anybody and everybody who has asked; and, given his proximity to Tinseltown and the unexpressed need of almost everybody in this goddamned town *to* be beaten, he's been *busy*. "I adjust attitudes. I'm a nice guy, but if I don't like you . . ." and you hear him go all kind of dreamy. "Well, Lou Thesz, if he didn't like you, he'd hook you, rip your knee apart, break your fucking ankle, or just crank, and he'd say, 'If you hear a crack and you're a class guy? At that point you let go.' I'm a disciple of Lou's. And Karl's."

Were they class guys?

"Haha, look, either one of these guys got a hold of you and you were dead in the water. They'd tie these modern-day guys into knots because they had a LOT of tools, because, let's face it, not all holds work on all people, but they'd use the nose, ears, hair as handles and hit you with armlocks, necklocks, head chancery, front facelock you, singles from the outside. Take the *kimura*. Karl showed me the double wristlock, which is what it was called then, but Lou had done this in the '30s, and Lewis before that. But because Karl taught it to the Japanese, he'd always ask me after that when he showed it to me, 'What do you think of my kimura?' And I'd say, 'It's a double wristlock, you schmuck.' It's kind of a running joke we've got going but the difference between how it is done then and now . . . and everyone thinks they know this, but how Karl and Lou and I do it is that we work in the wrist twist before cranking it on. There's NO flex room in it that way, and so when you lift, you snap the wrist, the elbow, and the shoulder."

Well, isn't it hard to find training partners if you keep breaking their wrists, elbows, and shoulders?

"Hahahaha," he laughs. "You only train with guys you like, then," and he then regales with further tales of tough: him with Bruce Lee ("A sweet guy with lots of parlor tricks but willing to learn grappling. I miss him"), him with Sugar Ray Robinson, Muhammad Ali, and the list goes on—Chuck Norris, Benny "The Jet" Urquidez, Gokor Chivichyan, now one of his top students and probably the sole bearer of the finishing-hold flame that LeBell got from Thesz and Gotch, as well as UFC competitor Karo Parysian, kenpo karate king Ed Parker, Hayward Nishioka, and Bill "Superfoot" Wallace, just to name a few.

And quizzing LeBell on the Hollywood types, he leaps on his other love, which is largely how he's paid the bills all these years: stunt work. "It all works together. The judo helped me with the high falls. And with the lack of fear. But I do it all: motorcycling, rappelling. I'm in that movie *Beerfest*, a movie that's just out [Sept. 2006]. I'm in the *Reno 911* movie that's filming now . . . they're chasing me on a motorcycle and I'm in my skivvies and they can never catch me."

When I inevitably ask him about the possibility of slowing down at seventy-four, he scoffs and says, "As long as I can still stretch someone who needs their attitude adjusted, well, I feel fine." And I can feel him looking at me, and of course I know as sure as the sun will rise and the moon will set that I'll find myself on the mat with him, pushing the variances of how far various joints were ever meant to go. He puts ten of his dollars up against ten of my dollars in an upcoming UFC matchup of Matt Hughes with one of the few men to ever beat him, B. J. Penn. (My money's on Penn.)

And when finally I ask who else he thinks is great, he names Dan Gable, whose 299 wins as an amateur and then, later, his wins as a gold-medaling Olympian mark him as one of the greatest this sport has ever seen. LeBell says, "Dan Gable is my hero, and the reason he is my hero is not only because he won an Olympic gold medal but I . . . because he is the most successful teacher that I've ever known. So even as skinny as he is, for me he walks on water. And when I grow up, I hope to be just like him."

Dan Gable

It was like a *leitmotif*, and its presence had started to exert itself, this weirdly insistent refrain, even before it had come out of anyone's mouth and took shape like a word. It was there when, cozied into my window seat on a flight to Iowa, I was asked by some guy if the blanket and pillow on his seat, the one next to me, were mine.

No.

"It's NOT yours?!" And there it was, full of incredulity, and more than this, a challenge.

"It comes with the seat," I say before pausing and watching where I might next go with this. "Or perhaps I am scampering about like Johnny Fucking Pillowseed, placing my personal blankets and pillows on *everyone's* goddamned seat. What the hell is wrong with you?"

Which, all in all, is probably not a bad way to begin a nine-hour, multiple-flight-change journey to the University of Iowa to track down one of the greatest living fighters in the world, self-described wrestler Dan Gable. In this age of aggressive hyperbole where the snarky among us might put quote marks around "greatest," I think we'll be glad to qualify this: 182 wins, 1 loss. Through high school. Through college. And goddamned straight into the 1972 Olympics, where he didn't surrender a point in six matches on his way to a gold medal that was almost an afterthought at that point. Is that great enough for you?

And it doesn't stop there. After moving into coaching, like a contagion he spread this Achilles-esque, kissed-by-God stuff to the University of Iowa, where he led their wrestling team to fifteen national titles in twenty-one seasons. Nine of these were won consecutively, between 1978 and 1986, and winning the Big Ten title every season as head coach, Gable's teams went UNDEFEATED seven times, garnering him a career coaching stand of 355 wins, 21 losses, 5 draws. No head for numbers? That's a .938 winning percentage.

Do you know what that means? Do you have ANY IDEA WHAT THAT MEANS? Sure, sure, doubting Thomases might invoke the Talent Attraction Principle, whereby the best want to work with the best and consequently remain the best, achieving nothing of great significance other than being in a place where all the great ones knew to go, but it's not that simple. Not nearly. Look at the Yankees. It's really not that simple. What this means, and I know it when I hear it and I hear it pretty soon after taking my seat in his office, is that, indeed, like the nostrum goes, it really isn't about winning. Not at all.

"There's a way to wrestle and be successful and win by putting out, sure," says Gable, leaning forward in his chair. "And there's a way to do that when you're putting out a little bit more." He pauses when he says these last three words *little . . . bit . . . more*, while his hands measure out in slow slices exactly what he means. "And eventually it gets even harder and it goes beyond. Beyond imagination. Beyond beyond. Most people can't even understand this. Unless you've been there. One thing's for sure: you can feel it on the other end. And when you felt it on the other end, what it did was it destroyed you. *That* is domination."

And that is the word that I hear that keeps coming up: *domination*. Dominate. Dominating. It's on sports gear I see around town, and while it never dawns on me until I see it that it might be a bit of collegial corporate catch-phrasery, it's been coming out of everybody's mouth ever since I said that I was coming here. To describe both the man, the team, *and* his style. And had his reputation not preceded him, I might have had a hard time seeing it sitting in this office in Iowa City, where he looks like nothing if not a sort of midwestern academic. But the whole story seems to be there in his eyes, eyes that are all at once kind and piercing, and in total it's not at all surprising to hear him finally say, when quizzed about his ONE loss to Larry Owings (a historical wrestling footnote, sort of the functional sports equivalent to former Beatle Pete Best), that "I analyzed it for a year. And for the next thirty years. I still analyze it. It ate at me so much."

Past tense? I'm not believing it.

"Well, it was just that I knew that it was because I wasn't capable of doing what I could have done. I wasn't thinking about me being undefeated and all of that either. I just wasn't focused on that match. And the interesting thing is that if he [Larry Owings] had to do it all over again, he wouldn't win that match. HE said that. He said that he could never get back to that level, that height. And for some reason that ended his career. But that match MADE my career. Not only up to and through the Olympics, but through my career as a coach."

So it wasn't the burden of your own legend that undid you there?

"Look, I didn't realize that something special was going on until I was in tenth grade. But it wasn't just all of the wins in competition that convinced me. It was just the amount of winning that I did everywhere. In practice, everywhere. There was no room for any other belief. I mean I never even thought about losing. You just knew you were going to win. And this is the difference: for me it had very little to do with the opponent. It had to do with me getting beyond beyond. I mean, I didn't think about them at all, and because of my reputation they probably didn't think of anything but me. And reputation becomes a winning psychological factor, but it still has to be supported by wins, and in my mind I couldn't lose. To anybody. That's what I felt. And I was beating everybody in all weight classes. It never mattered to me who I was fighting."

Todd Conner, author of a defining tome that looks inside the domination of wrestling by Iowa wrestling titled, in a stroke of marketing genius, *Domination: An Inside Look at Iowa Wrestling*, tells me about seeing Gable as a coach go up against two of his All-Americans, the dreaded Banach brothers, Lou and Ed, a heavyweight and a 177-pounder, respectively, at practice one day. "Now, Gable's 5'9" and probably weighed about 160 at the time. He was also about thirty-six years old. And first he crushed one and immediately afterward he crushed the other. Crushed." We enjoy a minute of quiet before turning back to watch the team practice.

The Hawkeyes' wrestling room reeks of new-mat smell and disinfectant. It's also two stories underground and like some wild Willy Wonka spread slathered with team colors, and at present a quorum of wrestlers are sitting patiently in the stands waiting for the AD to stop talking about paperwork and for Coach Tom Brands to kick things in. Brands, a three-time NCAA and Olympic champion, took over after the school gave the boot to Jimmy Zalesky, who took over after Gable retired. So Brands is in, with a crucial brand differentiator: now Gable is HIS assistant coach. Sort of like me having Nabokov as my proofreader, but Brands is no coach manqué and his opening speech starts kicking down the rails to him eventually screaming "NOW YOU ARE LIVING THE LIFE," and it feels the same way it feels when you're sitting up at the top of a rollercoaster.

Because no sooner is he done but warm-ups start, and then drills, and then a little live wrestling, and suddenly it is very nearly apparent that we're definitely not in Kansas anymore. At first I think it's that outside eyes are skewing the sampling and they're just going as hard as they're going because we're watching . . . until Conner tells me, "This is the first practice of the season, so they're going light today."

Their "light" would not only kill about everyone I've ever trained with who didn't go to school here but it's nowhere near the opposite end of things from "heavy." It's like Gable said . . . *beyond*. Or shadows thereof. It is, after all, the first day. But imagine, if you would, how you might train if I told you that if your effort level slipped below 98 percent, you'd be shot where you stood. Or if your hair was on fire. Or if you were caught slacking you wouldn't make the team and have to go back to de-tasseling corn stalks somewhere *else* in Iowa. They are properly motivated, and when I see one guy in the stands, I ask Gable what of.

"Oh. He's in the penalty box. It'd kill me if I had to spend even five minutes in there. "Hey," he starts to ask, "what'd you do?" And the kid, no more than twenty, with a long scar up his left knee, explains, with what seems to be genuine remorse, that he'd missed the requisite number of hours of study hall because he was training. And he sits for the entire three-hour practice, looking more morose as the minutes go by. Brands goes over moves, moves that even in demo mode he runs through like it's a life, and very possibly a death, situation. Which in a way it sort of is. Wrestling programs at universities all over the U.S. are losing ground (while all states but two, Mississippi and Arkansas, Gable guesses, have high school wrestling) while commercial interest in wrestling outside the Olympics is confined to the bullshit tights-and-turnbuckle kind.

Conner claims that the personality types drawn to the rigors of the sport—the dieting, the privation (since recuperation necessitates early bedtimes), the endless driving, driving, driving—are such that "they'd probably be in prison or dead if it wasn't for wrestling." Gable, though, who's been doing a fine job of hanging back and wandering the mat while offering minute adjustments and periodic corrections (he and Brands doing a good two-step), sees a rosy future, drawn in distinctly Gableian hues.

"Look, when all of a sudden a guy like myself can dominate a sport from the athletic level. The athlete level. And then you go into coaching and you can also dominate it. There are reasons somebody can dominate something, and if you look at one of the main reasons, if you look at any sport, you might want to look at . . . myself, or my athletes—not only did we dominate, but we drew attention, or crowds . . . is because there was more *entertainment* in the matches than a normal match. It wasn't all just fine art or fine skills. It was a harder style. These other sports that you're talking about here [boxing, mixed martial arts] are already hard. I made sport wrestling harder, and it became natural to me to be able to do that. And because it inflicted extraordinary amounts of pain and showcased the ability of some people NOT to hold up, all of a sudden what you have is, eventually, domination that functions as entertainment. This is really the oldest kind of human drama there is."

And as practice winds down and wrestlers start to filter out, Gable comes over and takes his final leave of me. "I gotta put some work in," he says, shakes my hand, and wanders off to the cardio area. He limps when he walks, two hip replacements and one that now needs to be redone, and I note that earlier, when he was showing me around, the thought had never seemed to occur to him to use the elevator in the four-story athletic building that housed his two offices and their practice and locker rooms.

"If you're tough enough . . . " he at one point had started to say to me, and I thought, before he even finished, "If." The whole world balanced on that *IF*. *IF you were tough enough*. And as I began to back out of the double swinging doors I started to wonder what it was like to live life beyond that *IF*. Beyond beyond. In the grips of some sort of transcendently evident desire to destroy, dominate, drive off into the ether your enemies like Gable had done in one international match where his opponent just left the mat before the match was over, just walked off of it still wearing his singlet, out of the door, a grand mal *no más*. IF you could harness that for a minute or a lifetime, to quote Kurtz (again), "Our troubles here would soon be over."

"You're welcome to come back anytime," Gable waved.

Oh, I will. Goddamned right I will.

THE BEST PROFESSIONAL-WRESTLING-BEFORE-PROFESSIONAL-WRESTLING-WAS-MUSCLE-BALLET FLICK

NIGHT AND THE CITY (1950) DIRECTED BY JULES DASSIN

Anybody what ever seen Richard Widmark push Victor Mature's wheelchaired mother down the stairs in the 1947 *Kiss of Death* knows if his name is on the marquee we're not talking paragons of virtue of any kind. Blacklisted director Jules Dassin's treatment of post-war pugilists, specifically professional wrestlers (before professional wrestling was all about tights, trash talking and T-shirt sales) was dead on. Bearing absolutely no resemblance to the book of the same name since the on-the-lam-from-McCarthy's-commie-witch-hunt Dassin had never *read* the book and improvised the script, which marginally follows Widmark's Harry Fabian through the rough and tumble world of fight promotion, noteworthy for two reasons and two reasons: Stanislaus Zbyszko and Mike Mazurki. Polish and Ukrainian, respectively, these two fighters were the real deal. Which means, in today's terms, that they could probably single-handedly have killed just about anybody in pro wrestling today with hooks, punishing holds, and submissions that form the solid basis of the forgotten art of catch wrestling, or what we call today submission wrestling. The rest of the plot that swirls around a sort of *What Makes Sammy Run?* hustler's brass ring swing is entertaining enough, but when Zbyszko slaps a head chancery on Mazurki (a early variant of the guillotine choke) if you've ever even been in the same *room* with one before, you start to fucking ache. Yeah. It's *that* good.

SO YOU'RE BEING CHOKED: WHAT'S IT ALL ABOUT, ALFIE?!?

Your first time? I mean the first time it happens will probably be remembered in the same way, that is, of course, if you can remember some, any, or even a small part of it afterward.

There'll be the sudden rush, the struggle (yours), and then the slow descent of cottony silence as the voices fade out and everything seems like you're looking through the wrong end of a telescope. The first time it happened to me it happened at the hands of Matt Furey. Though now widely derided by those in the know as sort of a quasi Billy Blanks exercise enthusiast, Furey was, and is, the real deal. After eight years of kenpo karate ("You might as well have been studying interpretive dance," he said), a year of muay thai, and a month of thinking about how another Gracie (Royce this time) had run through the competition in the first bow of what's now called mixed martial arts, no holds barred, or submission fighting, using this selfsame choke, I had asked him to show it to me.

After I came to, I asked, chagrined, "What do you do when they get you in one of these?"

"That's like asking 'What do you do after you've been knocked out?'"

Perfect. Perfect and perfectly helpless in a way that most of us haven't been since we were old enough to be able to tell on someone. It's a nightmare, and nightmarish, this inability to breathe, and if being able to avoid it was part of the holy and secret canon of crypto-martial artistry that would not be revealed to me until Furey revealed to me that he was indeed my father, Luke—well, fuck it. I'd try to figure out myself.

Enter, again, Dr. Steven G. Ballinger, M.D., Diplomate of the American Board of Orthopedic Surgeons and Fellow of the American Academy of Orthopedic Surgeons. He of the big brain might be able to help me to try to get my hands around what happens when there are hands around your neck.

I can't breathe and it's not a Heimlich issue. What do I do?

You got to understand nerves first off. Nerves are the greediest and most high-maintenance cells in the body.

Don't believe it?

Put a tourniquet around your arm and start pumping a rubber ball with your hand. Keep going. The first thing you notice is numbness. That's the sensory nerves shutting off. Then your power drops, and not because your muscle is burning and exhausted, but because your motor nerves are quitting. You can't keep going long enough to get your muscle to give up, because muscle doesn't mind running on low or no oxygen.

Look, anyone who has ever run a 440 has racked up a severe muscle-oxygen debt—when oxygen gets consumed faster than it is provided, glucose breaks down into lactic acid instead of carbon dioxide. Lactic acid is nasty stuff—it's what causes the muscle pain that makes you walk around like an old man the day after you start a new training program. Most tissue in the body is pretty tolerant of some lactic acid.

Not so neurons, the cells that nerves are made of. Even a slight drop in oxygen will create a net increase in lactic acid, and nerves suck up glucose and oxygen like a drag-racing Hummer sucks gas. Nerves are covered with little switches that will shut business right down if things aren't just right.

But _do_ . . . what do I do? I mean, relax to minimize the oxygen debt? What?

In hot weather a skinny girl will have a little bit of vasodilation, where the blood vessels in her skin open up a little so that blood can cool off under the sweaty skin, and BOOM. A little drop in the blood pressure to the brain creates an oxygen debt that makes her faint. There are six big arteries going to your brain, and four of them can be squeezed shut by a chokehold. Once the flow is decreased enough to let lactic acid build up—this amount varies from person to person—a chain reaction starts that will result in unconsciousness. If the neurons aren't working, they don't generate much lactic acid, and to prevent permanent brain damage, the brain does the only thing it can do to protect itself—it shuts off. It's just like a computer that has heat sensors that keep the computer from burning up if the fans quit working. Once the computer shuts off, it stops generating heat, and nothing gets fried.

Of course, once the brain shuts off, the neurons don't stop working completely; they still have to do some metabolizing, or they die. You can't just lie there without brain flow indefinitely—at some point, if the blood flow to your brain doesn't start up again, bringing oxygen and carrying off carbon dioxide, the cells _will_ start dying. How long this takes varies from person to person. In general, children and women do better for longer periods without blood flow. Men and old people do worse. So perhaps you could be a woman or a child, that might help.

Would that I were . . . but I'm not. Soooo. . . . ?

Well, a pretty good rule of thumb is five minutes. If someone has no brain flow for less than five minutes, they will probably wake up and be okay. More than five minutes, you got some 'splaining to do. It's possible to induce permanent brain damage in three or four minutes in a delicate person, like someone with severe diabetes or clogged carotid arteries. Then again, there are cases of children trapped under ice for more than fifteen minutes who ended up waking up and being pretty normal.

There is also evidence that going out for thirty seconds causes a little brain damage. Our brains are big and have lots and lots of redundant pathways—there are spare parts galore built in. If someone gets gorked and he wakes up with twenty percent of his redundant pathways damaged, he still can seem totally normal and remember his name and birthday and whatnot. Guys who get knocked out a lot, however . . . I've known a few gluttons for punishment, present company included, and over the years they definitely develop a certain behavior pattern that is probably due to critical loss of pathways. They talk loud, tell the same stories over and over again . . .

Would that I were . . . but I'm not. Soooo. . . . ?

Yes. Exactly. They seem drunk all the time, and may get clumsy; they develop a weird "overfriendly" personality and talk way too much about personal stuff that might best be kept secret. They also tend to get less intelligent and can't keep a job, or a pair of sunglasses, for more than a couple of weeks.

People who have had loss of brain flow for too long won't wake up right away after flow is re-established. This is true if the blood flow stops because their carotids were compressed by choking, or if their heart stops, or if they lose a bunch of blood and don't have any to pump to the head. This is what we call a "coma"—the brain has been damaged to the extent that it won't re-boot right away, and stays in idle mode to prevent further damage. Typically there is some swelling from damaged tissue and toxic buildup of lactic acid and other stuff. Once the swelling goes down and the bad chemicals wash away, sometimes people wake up again—but they are not the same.

Forget the TV plot device where someone gets knocked out for two hours and then hops up and kicks everyone's ass—that just doesn't happen. If someone is in a coma for a week or more, their brain is going to be very different after they wake up than it was before—not usually in a good way.

So much for Uma Thurman killing everyone after a long coma in *Kill Bill*. She would have been lucky to get a job emptying the trash at the Dollar Store.

NINE
I, SPARTACUS!

PAPER LION CHALLENGE #1: GETTING GHOLAR

At one point back in the '70s, it seemed the so-called pointy-headed Eastern liberal media establishment stopped trying to park a bicycle straight for a few minutes and went all crazy for the fistic arts. Joyce Carol Oates was writing about it, Norman Mailer was stepping into the ring to fight about it, and George Plimpton, with his whole *Paper Lion* deal, was doing it (along with every other sport/activity he could get his hands on). Valiant efforts all, but the Plimpton bug stuck, because, well, because it didn't take much to get into the ring with another writer. But it took a whole lot of stoneage to get into the ring with a pro.

How much?

Stones so big you'd break your neck if you fell off of them. THAT big.

And so it was that I got the idea: if George could do it, so could I. Of course, George is now dead, a point barely considered by me at the time I was having this think-tank-level of ideation.

"Well, it's your call, of course . . . but I don't know. . . ." The speaker was Todd Hester. The 6'4", 250-pound editor of, at the time, a premier mixed martial arts rag. "I don't know if I'd risk it."

Well, George did.

"I don't know . . . they might be good-natured to begin with. But at some point you're going to catch them with a punch that surprises them or stings or something, and if people are watching, they might just go ahead and break your arm or something just out of spite. Even if no one is watching, the last thing they want is to be shown up by a journalist who would then write about it and make them look silly. . . . I mean, their whole self-image and livelihood is tied up in their fighting, so messing with their egos might be a little explosive. . . . Just something to think about . . ."

I'm sorry, Todd. Did you say something? I didn't think so.

But I'm getting a little ahead of myself here. However, just let me say now in my present defense: the sun was in my eyes, I hadn't had breakfast, I was sporting a sore shoulder, the room was cold, the mat was uneven, and, finally, last but not least, I *could* have won.

I think.

I mean, if I really, really wanted to.

Especially if the good elves of the East sprinkled some more of that magical mystery dust on the doob I'd been smoking, I have absolutely not a single doubt in my mind that I'd be transported to a place where a mediocre fighter beats a pro. A place where speed means nothing. A place where Darrell Gholar, three-time U.S. Greco-Roman national champ, UFC scrapper, and International Cage Fighting king loses pitiably to Eugene Robinson.

Well, wherever *that* place is, it wasn't at the Beverly Hills Jiu Jitsu Club, where I, in the midst of this Bataan Death March of constant and continual beatings attempt to bring YOU, the reader, the best in front-row journalism. It was, however, where I met Gholar for this first in a series of ritual humiliations.

Gholar, as nice a guy as you'd want to meet, presuming you were meeting him someplace other than a mat, showed up on time and announced that he wanted to work out on the heavy bag before we started.

Big-balled move, I thought. But that's okay. Those with big balls all eventually lose, crashing down under the crushing might of the mighty. This was my pep talk to myself. A way to keep my mind off the fact that Gholar had beaten some of the best wrestlers in the world, earned Pan Am and World Championship honors, and even been an Olympic alternate, fer chrissakes. My pep talk ended with my memory of the last place I had seen Gholar in action: losing on Columbia TriStar Television's *Mad Max*–inspired *Battle Dome*. It was a performance I was hoping he'd repeat today.

At 5'8", 185 pounds, Gholar stood across the mat from me, who was stretching the tape at 6'1" and weighing in at 208 (down from an all-time high of 265).

"I'm going to try to win," I said, smiling through my mouth guard.

"Haha. Well, yeah. You should." Gholar laughed before we hit crunch time. We started slow, and, glancing up at the clock, I was priding myself on the fact that 35 seconds had gone by and I, get this, *was still in the game.* (Screw it, I'm willing to take my victories where I can get them.)

We locked up, over and under, and because of the whole Greco thing, I was on the lookout for upper-body controls to throws and was keeping my weight low. Gholar snapped loose and shot in for the single leg. Not to actually *get* the single leg but just to show me something I had heretofore been unaware of: his lightning quickness.

How fast was he? Fast enough that when I sprawled away from his double leg shot, he moved his body up and over me into a move that I hadn't been caught in in *years*. The guillotine choke. I escaped and we went to the floor and jockeyed for position. Gholar the whole time pressed his attack and easily defended against my guard, and almost everything else. I, not wanting to dog it, moved into a crouching Gholar at the same time that I felt the guillotine *again*. This time joined by a chin control hold. There was no escaping this, even with the arm over the shoulder, and, thinking that I might be able to outlast him (he had lifted me off the ground), I held on until . . . well, until the birds started to sing that song they sing whenever the end is near. *Tweet tweet, good night motherfucker.*

And that was it. Loser and still champion, indeed. The lesson learned? "Keep your head up," said Gholar.

PAPER LION CHALLENGE #2: HIS NAME WAS RICO

"You fought Gholar? I like his look. How was he?" The speaker was Rico Chiapparelli.

Yeah. Who?

Well, let's see if I can explain this to you by way of lineage: the greatest American wrestler EVER in the history of American wrestling (though there are whispers about those premodern-era guys like FRANK GOTCH, and some of the early professional wrestlers before the professional part of wrestling came to mean bullshit) was Dan Gable. Gable's record right before he won the gold medal for wrestling in the 1972 Munich Olympics was 299 wins, 6 losses, and 3 draws. His record as a coach, after retiring from competition himself, was 355 wins, 21 loses, and 6 draws, with 15 NCAA titles in 21 years.

Which means he's been around. Coached lots of wrestlers. Wrestled lots of wrestlers. Befriended even probably a greater number. He didn't have, purportedly, pictures of very many, or any, in his office at the University of Iowa, where he had coached, and now (after retiring, he's back as an assistant to one of his wrestlers who is now rocking the head coach job).

Chiapparelli's picture was on his wall.

Which is why I should fight him. For that reason, and that reason alone.

Yes, in a moment of madness, perhaps, I thought that the R1 Team Captain (*nee* Real American Wrestling, or RAW) Rico Chiapparelli, semi-retired and at a 40-odd pound weight disadvantage to me, might hand me my rock and roll fantasy win.

I'll pause here until you stop laughing.

Anyway, that's what I was doing walking up to RAW's El Segundo headquarters. Chiapparelli's *vita* was beautiful: three time All-American, NCAA collegiate wrestling, U.S. Open freestyle, and World Cup champ. Nickname? The "Baltimore Butcher."

Immaterial.

To me at least. I'd once heard someone say, "Even a blind mouse can find cheese SOMEtime." And watching the almost svelte Chiapparelli sitting on the apron of the ring, leaning into his girlfriend, I felt the first full flush of confidence and heard the whispers of the little voice that got me here in the first place. You know the voice that says: *Maybe.* As in, "Maybe you can kick his ass." Or, "Maybe today will be your day."

I'll pause here until *I* stop laughing. Bitterly. At my own insanity.

In any case, in chatting with Chiapparelli I was taken with not only his poise but his generally easygoing vibe. A genuinely nice guy. Shame that today must be the day that he loses to me, I thought. A thought I nurtured until we hit the mat and all thoughts of anything other than my crush-kill-destroy game plan were gone.

(At this point let it be noted for the record that this was the last thing that I DO remember. The rest of the story's been carefully reconstructed from photographs, eyewitness accounts, and, um, X-rays.)

Because my prefight plan had me thinking that guys with great technique don't do much else because they let the technique do the talking, I had decided to just wear Chiapparelli down. Muscle him, stymie him, whatever . . . to get him into fatigue mode.

As if.

We met in the middle and hit the mat. I have no idea how. Chiapparelli's flow would have made a raging river cry, and he slipped, at will, from my guard, on me, around me, almost through me. My most favored weapon— muscle strength—was a total non-issue since Chiapparelli never forced ANY of his attempts. If it didn't work (less the case) or he wasn't interested enough in a move to pursue it (more likely the case) he just kept going. Like a magician with a magic hat of plenty, Chiapparelli mixed the tricks and kept them coming.

In frustration, I made to stand us up again and escaped with almost everything. I say "almost" because he pulled me down and started spinning around in a motion that suggested an ankle lock, which was impossible, mostly because he didn't have my ankle.

Except he did.

Like everybody else who trains, there are just things that I don't get caught with anymore, and I don't think I had been caught in an ankle lock for YEARS. So imagine my surprise as Chiapparelli, smiling at me from the other end of my leg, just waited for the moment everybody but me had known to be inevitable.

Yeah yeah yeah, okay. I tapped.

And sitting on the mat in the stunned aftermath of what felt like a very SHORT fight ("It WAS."—Editor), I asked in this actual moment of doubt and pain the question I'm sure you're wondering about as well: Give it to me straight, Rico . . . do I suck?

This ain't an easy question to ask. It's like asking your girlfriend if you're the best she's ever had. If she answers too quick, she's lying. If she answers too slow, she's trying to not hurt your feelings.

On cue, and at the exact right time, Coach Extraordinaire Chiapparelli laughed and said, "I *expected* you to be really bad. But really you're not." Faint praise maybe but if I was man enough to ask it, I was man enough to have it answered, and anyway that's all I needed to get me back in the saddle.

PAPER LION CHALLENGE #3: A TALE OF TWO GRACIES

Daniel Gracie

"Autumn in New York is often mingled with pain."—Vernon Duke

Well, it was autumn, and, as will happen when seasons change, a young man's heart turns to fancies of vicious beatings delivered by the hands of brawny Brazilians, but that has us a little too far ahead of the story. Let's start at the beginning.

New York was calling from beyond the horizon, and so New York, proud sponsor of the World Freestyle Wrestling Championship, was where and what it would be. Standard city fare, veritable homecoming for a native like me: in other words, the whole nine yards of whirlwind travel and grappling galore. Including as an extra special added bonus attraction a visit to Renzo Gracie's place to fight him for your sordid amusements.

Well, at least that was the plan. And as the best laid plans of mice and men often fall asunder so it is that my calls to Renzo go unanswered; however, in a burst of inspired thinking I decide to just GO to him. Mohammed makes it over to the Mountain. Whatever. After a weekend of fighting I needed to fight and I knew someone there would fight me.

So for my sins I got to fight. And after it was over, to rip off several lines from *Apocalypse Now*, I'd not want another. Well, I mean, probably not.

Renzo's place sits in Midtown. Nondescript building and a guaranteed bracing by the doorman. It's then that you notice for the first time that there's no mention of the place where you're going on the building registry and the doorman then mutely thumbs you toward the basement. And moving over the concrete spread of stairs, stairs, and more stairs and through some steel-shanked doors, you finally step into that place that always feels like home to you if you fight: The Gym.

Renzo?

Not here yet. So I cop a seat on the floor and when he shows I start in on the explanation: "Eugene. . . . I called . . . and . . ." He starts apologizing for not returning my calls but I say I'm there to fight and talk to him and he says, smiling, all grace and ambassador-cool, "Well, get changed."

Later, while watching him train with cousins Ryan, Rodrigo, and Daniel, I start to have . . . not misgivings exactly . . . but maybe, well, yes, fine: misgivings. They were all as sharp as, uh, very, very sharp tacks and from drill to drill, the Gracies and other associated fighters, eyes all turned toward an upcoming PRIDE (a UFC-esque event), were ON.

Which was good for me. Renzo's fatigue spells Eugene's possible success. Especially if by success you mean only getting my head kicked in once versus again and again.

But as the clock turns and I eagerly await Renzo, he turns to me and says, "Warm up with Daniel first. I mean, fight him."

"Daniel?" Six-two, 243—*that* Daniel? Okay. Fine. I'm walking around 205 these days, so, fine. Daniel shrugs amiably and approaches me, smiling. "You ready?"

I think I mumbled "yes." In any case, whatever I said started it and there we were, tumbling down what felt like a very long hill.

And I was tapping my surrender all the way.

I tapped to a speedily applied arm bar.

I tapped to a choke.

I tapped to a heel hook.

I tapped to a smother.

And pretty soon I was just tapping to BE tapping. Not indiscriminately. I mean, not because I didn't HAVE to, because I DID have to if I wanted to leave there whole, but because after a while there was just no resisting the Big Three: superior strength, technique, and size. I was watching the world's smallest horror movie AND I was starring in it. If Daniel Gracie was supposed to be my freaking warm-up, I think it could safely be said that today's ritual humiliation had just begun.

Because even though his pro record was only 2-0 in PRIDE events, thirty-one-year-old Daniel, schooled by the man he describes as the greatest Gracie teacher ever—Renzo Gracie—Daniel moves like he is to the manner born and with surprising agility for a man that large. And maybe it's just that he's the

heaviest fast fighter that I've ever fought, but I start to feel like crucial measures are going to be needed if I'm going to be able to write this thing with even a scintilla of balance, and so in an explosion of concerted effort I actually succeed in getting him in some modified and spasmodic side controlled head chancery.

Genius.

And like with all forms of occasional genius, this was met with highly predictable results: me tap, tap, tapping on heaven's door.

Damn. It's then that I notice that he's chuckling. Choking me and chuckling. Out-maneuvering me and chuckling. So much chuckling that it's contagious and I start too. Pretty soon I'm laughing my ass off. Tapping AND laughing. Until this, a new wrinkle: I tap and he slowly shakes his head.

"What?"

"No, man. You can't tap to that."

"Well, I was just getting into the habit."

"Don't."

"So you want to start again?" I ask, almost begging for time.

"No. You did not tap. No tap. Just keep going."

And I did. Eyeing Ryan, who seemed to be waiting for his shot and searching for Renzo, who was now nowhere in sight.

As I lay there NOT tapping but getting twisted into a ball of extended pain I watched with curiosity as Renzo emerged from the locker room, dressed and refreshed. Going where?

"To lunch. Come on."

Yeah, yeah, I was supposed to fight him next. Yeah yeah yeah. Thank heaven for small freaking favors. Renzo, Daniel, Ryan, and a host of other fighters all hit the local steakhouse and replenished their depleted calories while Renzo talked about his upcoming fights, not the least of which was going to be my return match. Which I accused him of being afraid of.

"Anytime," he countered.

"Anytime I'm recovered from today's beating," I corrected.

Laughing, he added, "Anytime at all, man."

A gentleman and all-around great guy.

Too bad I was going to have to kick his ass when I came back.

Cesar Gracie: Coming Not to Praise Him

Cesar Gracie's joint up in Pleasant Hill, California, has pound for pound and square inch by square inch some of the world's best fighters in Dave Terrell,

Nick Diaz, Jake Shields, and Gil Melendez (see, "The Thrill of Undefeat, or, One Man's Peek into the Yawning Maw of Total Personal Failure and Its Transcendence Measured Out One Fight at a Time. Ladies and Gentlemen: Gilbert Melendez," in chapter 12). What is it that they say about those not doing, but teaching? Perhaps. I mean, could it be? Could it be that in a face-to-face challenge with my second Gracie, that I score in bigger and better fashion than before because, as the knock against Cesar goes, "Well, he's never really competed"? (It should be noted for the sake of future reference and my eventual longterm health that this was not a critique leveled by ME, however. Even after his 21-second loss to the great Frank Shamrock at the Shark Tank in San Jose.)

Well, there's a big goddamned difference between NOT competing and not being ABLE to. Cesar, in a lot of ways—chip on his shoulder, something to prove, just being plain ol' sick and tired of the knocks—COULD be the most dangerous of the Gracies, because a man trying to make a point is always dangerous. And if he trained anything like he coached, I'd be in for a hard ride.

RECALL: Ringside at WEC, Gil Castillo is fighting, and over my shoulder Cesar and Chris Sanford (a.k.a "The Only Man to Ever Knock Me Out") are screaming words of encouragement. Sort of.

"WHAT'S THE MATTER WITH YOU?!?!?"

"YOU GOTTA REALLY THINK ABOUT GETTING YOUR LIFE TOGETHER!"

"WHERE THE HELL ARE YOUR PRIORITIES?!?!"

And when a clearly dispirited Castillo returned to his corner after a completely underwhelming second round (you think?) he returned to a corner full of air. Nothing. No one. To paraphrase what my mom used to tell me, "When you win, the world wins with you, when you lose, you lose alone." Cesar and Chris were gone, and THAT'S the hard school, a.k.a. The Fuck-You Fight School of Training.

Hard man. And like my kid once said to me when I was contemplating training with this boxer who had killed no fewer than TWO people OUTSIDE of the ring: "Are you sure you want to do this?"

I wasn't, but there I was, up at this guy's school and in the midst of an interview with him and listening to that devil in my head that was saying like he always says: "LOOK at him. He's not so TOUGH. I fucking KNOW you could take him. You could KICK . . . HIS . . . ASS."

And these completely unwholesome and horribly, horribly misleading thoughts continue right up until the time that we change into fight gear and put mouthpieces in and get into the ring and I check his game face.

Jesus.

Okay. Yeah, it's business and nobody's going to let some smarty-mouth journalist into the ring and walk out with a victory story, but you know what? A hard look never hurt anybody, or so I keep telling myself when we lock up mid-ring. And there I got my first surprise.

At about 5'10" and 185 pounds, Cesar is clearly the smaller man, though that never stopped, say, a Frank Trigg from rushing me. But my first surprise is the master's touch that Cesar brings to bear: he waits. His breathing is even, level, and he parries and side steps, switches grips, all with ease. So much ease that I get angry. Something, despite all of the talk about the art in martial arts, WILL happen, and I start manhandling him. Go for a guillotine despite knowing it won't work on him and we go to the ground and he starts spinning and I start pulling everything in the house. Arms tight and he goes tighter, and while I'm thinking strength, strength, strength, and muscling him to go God knows where, he swivels around so fast and smooth that I almost don't have a sense not only of where it's coming from but where it's going.

But pain is a wonderful tour guide and as he extends facedown on the mat and I feel my arm extend with him (the same arm that I should have kept tighter . . . and done so faster), I think: Goddamn it, of COURSE. And I tap and sit up and everyone previously watching looks away. Sadly. Soooo sadly.

Hahah. Fuck that. In the crucible of my failure is a greater soul forged!!!! And besides which, I can still beat Rollins, Danzig, Evan Seinfeld, and just about everyone ELSE in music, my real field of play, with the possible exception of RAY CAPPO, he formerly of YOUTH OF TODAY who has been training for the last ten years under one of the masterful Machados. But fuck it, I'll take my loss to Cesar like a man and keep the whining, crying, and blaspheming to a bare minimum. Today.

TEN

SO YOUR EAR'S BEEN BITTEN BY MIKE TYSON....
ONE SURVIVOR'S TALE

It was the sport's equivalent of Pearl Harbor. Where were you when, in the middle of a major televised sporting event, the former heavyweight champion bit, not once but twice, the ear of his heavyweight challenger, and then spit it out?

I was in an Irish bar with a roomful of suddenly silent Irishmen. It was one of the single most stunningly telling televised moments I'd ever had a chance to be part of.

It was not the sports nadir that so many hand-wringing businessmen who were concerned about "what this might mean for the sport" thought. It was a real and true moment of honesty wherein, Zeus-like, a competitor's desire to move beyond competition into the whole elemental *consumption* thing was acted on.

Since then, since that fall and the rape conviction that precipitated it and the subsequent years in the wilderness, wandering and wondering, Tyson pops up on the periphery of my consciousness, as well as my person: sitting next to me at the AVN awards show in Vegas, where porn stars jostle for a chance to be photographed with the murmuring Tyson; or suddenly flanking me in the media row at the Ultimate Fighting Championship, where I find myself standing between him and The Rock. And our conversations always seem the same, with him blankly mumbling consent to some entreaty to "do a piece."

And while it was and sort of remains convenient to bifurcate our understanding of how this all played out in black and white with the biter, Tyson, the villain, and the bitten, Evander Holyfield, the victim, what a difference a day makes. Or an athletic commission ruling.

In August 2005, the *New York Daily News* dropped a blockbuster: the New York State Athletic Commission banned the forty-two-year old Holyfield from boxing in New York, regardless of his passing a raft of required tests.

Boxing loves its conspiracies. Was it the fact that Holyfield was never the company guy, paddycaking it with the goodfellas over at HBO? Was it the short-order losses to the likes of Chris Byrd (who?) James Toney, and then Larry Donald (who? WHO?)? Or was it a public aversion to watching a now-old man flame out like some wasted, punchy and pencil-pushing pugilist?

Who knows? What *was* known was that all through the ear-biting imbroglio nobody had really asked him about it because they felt like they had already seen it. Fools.

That's where I come in. Driving through the monogrammed gates of Holyfield's palatial digs in Fairburn, Georgia, it seemed to me that none of the usual questions that you might ask someone who had suffered ear avulsion at the hands of a bipolar ex-con ("Were you afraid? How afraid? Like crap-your-pants afraid?") really applied, especially when the bipolar ex-con had been in the process of getting his ass handed to him.

Then, standing in the entryway to his place, a surreal scene-by-scene remake of Tony Montana's spread from *Scarface*, I make my way to the living room and I ask him the only way I know how.

Tyson?

"Look, Tyson is a good example of a guy that they used to promote because he had talent but didn't know the game. And if you don't know the game, they prostitute you. If you know the game, they want to get you out of there and get somebody else young and stupid. To make money off of him."

Holyfield's a solid chunk, even allowing for age.

"So they promoted Mike and made him bigger than life because when Mike came to town everybody got paid. They did the same doggone thing to Ali. It's almost like they got *paid* to call him the greatest, and that was because they were ripping him off. They're still ripping him off. I guess he allows it because he wants them to love him."

Minus the ripping-off part some might have accused Holyfield of similar desires for public acclaim, given his resistance to the ban and his continuing to fight in off-market places like Dallas, where he faced a so-called insurance salesman and Kentuckian Jeremy Bates (who?) on August 19, 2006. (Holyfield was victorious—ref stoppage, round two—in a fight that Scott Kelly from Combatmusicradio.com called "a sad and horrifying work [unevenly matched fight, possibly fraudulent] that nonetheless showcased the talents of a great fighter.")

But the ear.

You know in both of your Tyson fights I think you used dirty tricks. I think you just didn't get caught. You were head-butting. You were wrestling, hitting after the bell, and so on.

And there it is. A little salt. I sit back on his cream-colored couch and watch him grow more animated than he's been the whole time I've been here.

"Wrong. Absolutely wrong. He was jumping off of his feet to head-butt me. My head was just harder than his. My attitude was 'That's what you get, sucker.' I don't go into no game cheating, but if you do it to me, I'm going to do it back to you.

Did it hurt?

"Yes."

And the breakdown of the post-bite surgery and so on and I'm only half listening because an idea is percolating. In my head.

Do you have a training ring here?

I mean it did not seem that there was anything that the house did not have. There had to be a ring there. But even though I was asking, he was clearly not telling.

Where do you train when you're here?

"Why?"

Well, out with it.

I figured you and I could go one three-minute round. You know, just for fun.

He laughed, stood up, and walked into a smallish bathroom off the living to take a leak. I could hear him chuckling, and he was still chuckling as he came out after straightening his clothes.

Hey, I train too. I'm a COMBAT ATHLETE, JACK!!!

"Look, I'll give you a ride to wherever you need to go."

I'll just write that you were afraid to fight me if you don't.

And again he chuckled. I wasn't quite so sure whether I should be a skosh offended at his complete refusal to take my challenge seriously, or thankful. But as we wended our way through Atlanta traffic, with him waving after well-wishers, fight fans, and the starstruck, he got to a part in the conversation where he started to demonstrate to me how the combinations another fighter was throwing at him were coming in.

And as I sat and watched his hands, I knew in that moment that if I was to move my hands as fast as humanly possible, for ME, to demonstrate the same thing, there's no way I could move them THAT fast. Add in him squared up across from me, and his twenty-plus years in the fight game, I see that I narrowly averted a large-scale personal national tragedy. To wit: a savage beating that sees me getting savagely beaten. Because if I did well, I'd shame him into giving me one. If I didn't do well, as many might predict, I'd be shamed into FORCING him to give me one. Thank goodness neither happened, I think, in honest appraisal. He'd have killed me. Unless . . . and here's the fatal flaw that fuels those one-too-many-drinks-for-their-own-good guys when they see guys like Holyfield out and about . . . unless I somehow took him down to the ground, where my real skills lie.

Yeah. Unless. If. Maybe.

The road to hell is paved with suchlike words.

Setting my bags on the curb, I notice him unconsciously rubbing his ear with the one hand as he waves me off with the other. And I take a last look at it.

Yeah. It makes sense. Tyson-esque sense, but sense nonetheless.

I coulda been a contender.

TEN BEST
BOXING MATCHES
IN HISTORY

(THE CHEAT SHEET TO HELP YOU FAKE LIKE YOU KNOW A FEW THINGS ABOUT A FEW THINGS)

1. Joe Louis v. Billy Conn, 1941: In my household Joe Louis was always pitied, and his plaintive, possibly apocryphal, post-fight cry of "I'm glad I won, Momma" was the signature of a champion who died almost undone by business and his inattention to it. But back in 1941, if you watch the film, Louis, who ended his career with 68 wins, 3 losses, and 54 knockouts, stumbles the entire fight until he delivers a right upper-cut quickly followed by a salvo of rights and lefts to Conn's head. And these were rights and lefts with those tiny friggin' gloves they used to use when fighters ended up selling pencils on street corners from brain damage after their careers were over. And finally: the right that put Conn to sleep in the 13th round. Classic come-from-behind win from a champion whom many had wanted to declare dead. Greatest heavyweight of all time? Goddamned right.

2. Gene Tunney v. Jack Dempsey, 1927: Jack Dempsey, history books have finally indicated, was a motherfucker. In that same motherfucker class that included Ty Cobb, and in which some would include the car wreck that "Iron" Mike Tyson's become, Dempsey tarried with gangsters, routinely attacked women, and took seri-ously his standing as one of the toughest men in the world. To wit: he did exactly what the fuck he wanted. Except at Soldier Field in front of 100,000 fans when Tunney, after a questionably long count, came back to give Battlin' Jack what all. Though Dempsey was later decried as being "old" and "soft," this fight was more good because of the snapshot it took of a fighter in decline than for any show of boxing bril-liance. Like *Bang the Drum Slowly*. But for boxing.

3. Muhammad Ali v. George Foreman, 1974: There's a reason so many movies have been made about this fight. Movies made, books written, column inches inked, all in the name of what everyone thought would be sport-sanctioned murder. I watched it on a Zenith TV in Brooklyn and from halfway around the world my mind was still blown: rope-a-dope? God-damned right. Ali redeems himself for his highly questionable and career-besmirching win over the compromised Sonny Liston.

4. Sugar Ray Leonard v. Tommy Hearns, 1981: Right after this? Yeah: exactly when boxing started its long march into total sports insignificance brought about by greed, confusion, and general stupidity. Leonard wins with a 14th-round TKO, not the way we like our fights to end (we of the rock-'em sock-'em class), but a great study all around, and a reminder of how good Leonard was/is.

5. Rocky Marciano v. Jersey Joe Wolcott (I), 1952: After getting his ass handed to him by the bigger and apparently tougher Wolcott (he who had laid low Joe Louis one time when) for the ENTIRE fight, Marciano came back with one right hand that said it all at 43 seconds into the 13th round, spinning Wolcott's head around like a top and ever so solidly removing the crown from that head upon which it sat. Look up "gutted out: win" and you'll see Marciano's face somewhere there.

6. Julio Cesar Chavez v. Meldrick Taylor, 1990: I started loving Chavez when, late in his career, on his way to his much-vaunted, much-wanted 100 fights, he fought some bum named Hagen. Hagen, in trying to generate some heat for a fight no one cared about, started taunting Chavez, making the claim that to get to 100 fights he must have fought a whole passel of Tijuana taxi drivers. The normally bloodless Chavez, rather than putting Hagen down right away, as it became clear he patently could have, kept him standing the whole match just so he could punish him and punish him and then punish him some more. After the beating had subsided, and Hagen admitted in a post-fight interview that they "must have been [some] pretty tough cabdrivers," Chavez had earned a place in my heart. This fight was no different. Though covered by the taint of confusion that marked boxing in its decline (Taylor clearly won the first eight rounds), Chavez's dogged and continued attack during the last rounds made this a good 'un. Like Scorcese good. Tough cab drivers, indeed.

7. Archie Moore v. Yvon Durelle, 1958: We love this one simply because we love the spectacle of old age getting after youth. The almost 45-year-old Moore against the 29-year-old Durelle fought this fight when fighters fought fights: Durelle's record was 81 wins, 20 losses, and 2 draws, Moore's was 173 wins, 22 losses, and 9 draws. Most of us will never do ANYTHING significant 173 times, much less win something, and so it was with great joy that I've watched (time and time again) Moore knock down the game Durelle, time and time again, before pulling out a totally tough win in round 11. Age before beauty, baby.

8. Marvelous Marvin Hagler v. Tommy "The Hitman" Hearns, 1985: This fight had such seismically significant ripples that one need but look at the aftermath to track its later trajectory: Hagler subsequently decamps to Italy, never to return; Hearns gets picked up in 2006 on a domestic rap for fistfighting with his son at home. (Over? Maybe who was going to take out the garbage?) But the first round of this fight is the most brutal many of us will ever see, and when Hagler wins it in round 3 you're almost relieved, like YOU were the one getting your ass kicked.

9. Riddick Bowe v. Evander Holyfield, 1992: Forget the later ear-biting debacle, forget the Bible-beating and his late-in-winter refusal to acknowledge that the circus has pulled out of his town, Holyfield and Brooklyn bomber Bowe fought a fearsome threesome of fights that stand (the Fan Man, the lunatic who parachuted into the ring in the middle of the fight, debacle aside) as some of the greatest ass kicking ever.

10. Muhammad Ali v. Joe Frazier (III), 1975: Frazier said before the fight that he was prepared to die in that ring. Ali said afterward that it was the closest to death he had ever come. Well, death took a holiday this night, but what Ali had proclaimed "a killa and a thrilla and a chilla" when he got "the gorilla in Manila," showed two consummate endurance artists fighting forward and clearly choosing not to quit, and they didn't. The fight was called when a merciful Frazier corner, Frazier himself with his eyes swollen shut, called the fight. Standing to celebrate, Ali passed out from exhaustion. Balls. In great evidence.

FIGHTING LIKE A GIRL

"I guess I just didn't play well with others," she laughs, her voice a light trill.

She?

Yeah, Kelsey Jeffries, the Road Warrior, the IFBA featherweight (126 pounds) world champ, the IBA super bantamweight world champ, the WIBA intercontinental super featherweight champ, and the WIBF America's Featherweight champ. *That* she.

You know, the she who labors on in relative obscurity, trying to make her bones at a day gig as a firefighter because, ironically, chances are you're probably much more familiar with Michelle Rodriguez's star turn as a "girl" boxer in 2000's *Girlfight* or more famously Oscar-winner (and former Karate Kid) Hilary Swank's Oscar-winning *Million Dollar Baby*, than you are with Jeffries' past twelve years in the ring.

Doing the math, that's twelve years, 53 fights (44 as a pro), 34 wins, a few KOs, and all of it summing up to a few pressing realities: tough things come in small packages, is one of them. Her being able to kick your ass is another.

"I was pretty introverted, I had issues at home, I was athletic, and I grew up a white girl in Hawaii. So I started fighting early," says the thirty-year-old fighter. And while the incongruity of beaches and brawls works its way around your head and you hum "Blue Hawaii," know that there's a whole other side to the beach culture that readily and quickly asserts itself in face of the fact that while Hawaii *is* part of the union, it's also a completely different country. A country where being a 5'4" strawberry blonde might be viewed as an invitation to remind a minority that they live in the only state in the union that has a majority that's non-white.

"But it was all tough," Jeffries laughs. Kind of. "I was what they called a *tita*. It's a Hawaiian word, or a Samoan word, for a fighting spirit, I think." And so from the beaches to three years of karate and a chance meet with Dennis Alexio (super heavyweight kickboxer with a pro record of 70-2 with 65 wins by knockout or TKO) at Gold's Gym, Jeffries started swinging through territory that, though discovered, has hardly been charted. Or at least not discovered enough to afford its pioneers limos, jewels, and a TV talk show on ESPN.

"Well, it was tough, because there were no women at any of these gyms. So I had to be tough because if I'm training with guys, which I did, and do, there's no way that they're going to let me beat them. I mean, if the average person trains at maybe seventy-five percent when they train I was probably always training at one hundred percent because I was training with guys who were training one hundred. Just to not get beaten by me."

Did you ever manage to kick any of their asses? Completely? Totally? Humiliatingly?
"No. I am too smart for that. If I could find a man I could beat, what would I gain from that?"

And then it dawns on us, that she's in an interesting place in space: she's fought both men and women. In the ring. Not over a kitchen table or something. Is there a difference? I mean, outside of the fact that most men would rather die in the ring than be publicly seen losing to a woman (and they fight like it when they do)?

All things being equal, how'd the experiences compare since from the outside, women's fights, like all lighter-weight fights, seem both faster *and* meaner?
"The biggest difference is one that's obvious. The power thing. This is a big difference."

So what kind of adjustments does the smaller fighter make when fighting a larger fighter?

"Well, I know I'm only going to win that one thinking-wise. And skill-wise. So I try to not get hit and play defense, defense, defense. Which in terms that the average person can understand means lots of head movement, lots of foot motion, which means moving my body. And then mostly I just box. Not fight, but BOX. Most of my fights have been won by decision. And I fight above my weight class as well."

Have many been lost by knockout?

"I've been dropped four times in my career. All from punches I didn't see. Which means southpaws. Fighting a southpaw is like dancing with a bad dance partner. The angles are all wrong and it's just not easy. But that's a Hollywood thing. Generally, in real life, women are not knocking people out. Mostly because knockouts come from fighters fighting fighters that can't really fight. Look at it 99.99 percent of the time if someone's got a record heavy on knockouts you really need to look at who they knocked out."

Spot quiz: *Girlfight* or *Million Dollar Baby*—which movie was better from a fight perspective?

"*Girlfight*. It was a better movie. More realistic." And working with Al Ramirez as a boxing coach and spending time training with Buddy McGirt, and fighting everywhere and anywhere she can get her hands on one, Jeffries' dance card, as drawn by the old New York salt Bruce Anderson, has her hitting the bricks old-school style.

"She's fought in Oregon, Washington, California, Mexico, New Jersey, Florida, Texas, Gdansk, Poland, Berlin, Nevada, Indiana . . . " Anderson's voice trails off. "That's why we started calling her the Road Warrior."

"Well, my manager likes for me to remain as the Road Warrior," says Jeffries. "But being from Hawaii I always like to include some Aloha/Hawaiian strength somewhere. *Ali'i* is a leader, great one, chief, officer, king, or in my case, queen. So *Ali'i* Warrior. I think you get the idea. It took me my entire career as the Road Warrior to achieve and earn the status of *Ali'i*. On my fight skirt I wear *Pu'ali*, which means warrior. I also go by *Pukaua*, which means fighter. It's something I know and no one else knows."

"Ali'i Warrior—confuses yet another," Anderson opines.

And finally I wonder aloud if being a bona fide ass kicker upends the delicate balance that's maybe overly reliant on her bearing the mantle of the weaker sex.
"What?"

Well, in nature, anthropologically speaking, it seems that males and females of a species that are more often more evenly matched in terms of size and strength are usually monogamous.
"Um . . . "

What I mean to say is, are you finding that being a killer makes your close personal relationships into something more like uneasy truces . . . like when you go home for Thanksgiving or something?
"I'm the baby in the family. But what I do for a living never comes up."

No older brothers playfully slap-boxing you around the holiday table?
"No. They never talk about it. They don't joke about it. I mean, not even a joke."

And I try to envision this weird sort of détente where what you know, as a sort of signpost of what you can do, is enough to back them up off of you. Actually *try* has very little to do with what I envision since I'm not being entirely honest here because at 6'1" and 225 pounds I know goddamned well what it feels like.

But I wonder if it's a heady, intoxicating sensation for someone who is not used to having it. Like you woke up one day to discover that you actually *were* Napoleon, or something. Or whether the crown is worn much more lightly, much more effortlessly, than it might seem to us lesser-gifted mortals. And as I listen to her, her voice, and the edge in her voice that creeps in as we get closer to when it's time for her to start training, I don't wonder too much anymore, as after a certain point it seems like asking someone with black hair how it feels to have black hair.

"Mahalo, my brother," she says by way of exit, and *this* I know. And as I say "you're welcome," she heads out to get ready for a September 14 bow* against a revolving door of opponents who "keep changing," according to Anderson, all Burgess Meredith aplomb, "because they're afraid to fight her or don't think they're getting enough money to get beaten by her." He sighs, and his sigh says, if I'm hearing it correctly, what he then very directly affirms: "Being number one is tough, but it's much better than not being number one."

Kelsey won by TKO in the 4th round.

A FIGHT FILM THAT WORKS ONLY IF YOU DON'T FIGHT, NEVER KNEW ANYBODY WHO DID FIGHT, OR BELIEVED ME WHEN I TOLD YOU THAT THE WORD "GULLIBLE" IS NOT IN THE DICTIONARY

BODY AND SOUL (1947) DIRECTED BY ROBERT ROSSEN

I'm not out to make any friends. That much should be clear. And taking a shot at ol' Johnny Garfield (who was nominated for an Oscar for his take on a prizefighter), with apologies due to Andy Applewaite, the biggest John Garfield fan I know, is almost necessary if you manage to move out beyond the penumbra of Hollywood's magical glow. A glow that has the perfectly-believable-as-a-gangster Garfield, standing up in this Oscar-winning flick, playing Charley Davis, a prizefighter tilting against the Mob and coming out The Winner. You think it works this way in real life? Well, we got a bridge in Brooklyn, or a hotel room in Vegas, that Sonny Liston could sell you, if so. Yeah, this film looks great, all noir-ish sheen and great editing, but the fact is not changed that nowhere is the gap wider between fighting and acting like you're fighting than here. Remember, just moving your boxing-gloved hands does not a fight make.

THE PHYSICS OF FACE PUNCHING

The movie was Guy Ritchie's *Lock, Stock and Two Smoking Barrels*. The scene was this caper-esque discovery by some robbers of a poorly placed meter maid. Or meter man. Or whatever the hell they're called. When the meter man regains consciousness after being head-butted into the un- side of the whole conscious-ness equation, one robber says to the other, "Knock him out." And they sort of stare at each other and the other one says, "Knock him out?"

It was a great set piece because the reality of it is most people have no idea not only how to knock someone out, but why they get knocked out ("From get-ting hit on the head a lot?"), or what happens *when* they get knocked out.

For this we went again to Dr. Steven Ballinger, whose qualifications as an orthopedic guy are beyond reproach and who holds the enviable title of "Strongest Hands in the County." The county? Camarillo, home of the mental institution made famous by Charlie Parker, Zappa, *and* Dr. Steven Ballinger, a former wrestler par excellence (hence the honorary title). We decamped to his

digs in Eastern Texas, and, fired up by the spirit of Plato (and Socrates and Glaucon), decided to find out what happens when the lights go out. For the purposes of those fans of *The Republic*, Dr. Ballinger will be playing Socrates, and I myself will be playing the taciturn toady Glaucon.

Is it not true that essence precedes existence with regards to face punchitizing?
"Well, the amount of damage inflicted by a blow to the face is related to a number of factors; foremost are the force of the punch and the area of the face that the force is spread over. Force can be estimated by using a simple equation, or by observing a well-delivered blow directly. When a punch is optimally delivered by a fighter standing on a stable base, slow-motion analysis will show a very slight backward movement of the fighter delivering the blow, and a complex mix of movements in the one receiving the lick. Force equals mass times velocity squared, so in the best scenario the force of the blow must be a little greater than the inertial mass of the puncher, hence his slight backward motion despite a wide base and good traction."

I concur. But what of the size differentialistics?

"Look, the equation is force equals mass times velocity *squared*. That is why a smaller guy with a fast fist can hit as hard, or harder, than a huge, slow guy—the velocity is squared, and the force increases logarithmically as velocity of the fist increases. Increasing the mass of the fighter or holding a roll of quarters in your fist only increases the force of the blow linearly—if the mass is doubled, the force is doubled. If the velocity of the fist is doubled, the force is quadrupled ($2 \times 2 = 4$, Einstein). If you have a choice of guys lined up in order to hit you in the face, and one is twice as big as the other but the little guy is twice as fast, which should you choose?"

The guy without the gun.

"Very funny. And while largely correct, in the spirit of this discussion, fairly useless. Okay, a big guy of mass 100 kg and fist speed of 5 meters/second will deliver a blow of 2,500N, but a little guy with body mass 50 kg and fist speed 10 meters/second will deliver a blow of 5,000N! Add to that, the smaller guy's fists are smaller, so the blow is concentrated on a smaller area, and it's easy to see how some of the most heinous thrashings in history came at the hands of an average-sized man."

I understand that Tojo had a hell of a left hook.

"Once the fist hits you, the amount of damage you take is also related to a number of factors. Taking the blow in a relatively soft place, like your fleshy jowl or cheek, diffuses the force of the blow radially and absorbs some of its power. When the blow lands far from your center of gravity or in a pendant structure (easily moved, like your head), some of the energy of the blow will be lost as rotational force, whipping your head around or knocking your jaw back. Getting knocked off your feet will also soak up a bunch of force and can protect your brain from injury (as long as you don't land on your head in the street, immediately cashing the force check good fortune has written you). If your jaw, tooth, or eye socket fracture (or if you are lucky—your nemesis's hand fractures), much energy will be absorbed by the bone breaking. Once that is done, however, all of the residual force will be translated into a shock wave that rattles your brain.

"You see, the brain floats in the skull like a yolk in an egg. When a rapid, intense force is applied to the skull, one of several things will happen. If the force is concentrated in a small area, the skull will fracture, like when an egg is struck with a hammer. If the force is diffused enough for the skull to resist cracking, the whole skull will move. The faster the skull is accelerated—here we see the importance of velocity *squared* again—the more likely the floating brain's protective system will be overwhelmed. The inertia of the brain floating in the skull will keep it still while the skull moves: hydraulic pressure will dissipate some of the force while fluid displaces from between the brain and the rapidly approaching skull wall.

"If the force is sufficient, all the fluid will get squirted to the sides and the brain will be smashed up against the wall. Blood vessels on the side of the brain away from the blow will get stretched and rupture, producing bleeding on the side opposite the punch. The brain will then rebound, sloshing back to the other side of the skull, and if there is still enough energy left after the brain tissue has absorbed its share, the blood vessels on the side of the brain that got smacked up against the wall get torn off as well. The brain will continue sloshing back and forth, ripping blood vessels and smashing tissue into pulp until the energy of the blow is all used up. The sudden deformation and jolt to the brain will interrupt nerve conduction, and the system crashes. And reboots. *If* you are lucky. If you aren't lucky your skull fills up with mushy brain tissue and blood clot, you die with one or both pupils blown wide and your body jerking like a worm on a flatiron."

You must be great at parties, Doc.

ELEVEN

SO YOU'VE BEEN BEATEN UP. . . .

OR, WHAT THE HELL ARE YOU LOOKING AT? PART 2

The old blues standard said it best: Nobody loves a loser, and on our po-mo flipside it seems everybody, and we mean freaking everybody, loves a winner. The whole Church of the High Five sings hosannas for the returning victors all pumped with the momentary glory of having TOTALLY KICKED ASS. From the 1950s lovable loser Charlie Brown to the 1990s Kurt Cobain variant, the truth will be proclaimed: hangdogism is now dead. Welcome to the decade of The Winner.

Yeah. Whatever.

An ass-kicking, like Fame, is a capricious bitch, and so it is that we celebrate the joy of getting, giving, loving, and living the Delicate Science of the Head Whipping.

SCENARIO NUMERO ONE

You step away to take a leak and in your absence a much larger, handsomer, and probably better-hung man presumes to take your:

1. stool
2. your drink
3. your girl
   and/or
4. all of the goddamned above

You return and:

A. Call the cops?
B. Pretend you're gay?
C. Say "So long, sister, you're on your own"?
   or
D. Slap his drink out his hand and fuck him up.
   orrrr
E. Get your ass kicked. One or the fucking other.

Answer Key

A. Like Travis Bickle said, "The cops don't do nothing, you know that." Cops, it should be noted, were also the guys who bounced your head off of the lockers in high school. Just because they operate under the color of authority doesn't mean they still don't secretly wish to do the same.

B. A workable solution. Though, it should be noted, you might still catch a beating.

C. Probably the best in the long run, because, after all, where the hell was that relationship going anyway?

D. and E. This cuts to the heart of a thought process that takes nanoseconds, and your brain—like a computer amped by Dutch courage, and what you're hoping is some sort of element of surprise, and really damaging film precedents (*Rocky, Raging Bull, Bloodsport*)—switches on the animal. Good. The damaging effects of having to live life under the aegis of having crawled AWAY from this fight will haunt you a lot longer than the actual pain from the beating. But let's examine why this is the best choice.

It's Not So Bad

Bar fights are typically fought by drinkers. That is, drunks. So play the odds— Stretch Armstrong might actually be drunker than you. The limitations of indoor fights can't be underestimated either. An errant bar stool either swung or tripped over can be your best friend. And positing the existence of friends of some sort, you might also count on the quick breakup, which leaves you free to posture, scream imprecations, and hope to God nobody takes you seriously and lets you go.

But if you want to fight to win, consider:

The Knee to the Head: Most people never think of this because your knee seems so far away from his head. Most people haven't studied the deadly Southeast Asian art of Muay Thai. Wrap your hands around the back of his head, yank down with an authoritative snap, and leap upward, knee first. As you leap, your downward snap will meet the rising of your knee, and when his head and your knee meet? Well, it's nothing sort of magic.

DRAWBACK: If you miss you'll probably end up leaping into his arms à la Jerry Lewis. NO ONE will think it's funny. Except maybe the French.

Choose Your Battles

You want to lose a fight? Fucking pick one. Every single fight I've picked (unless you're fighting a Frenchman who, given historical precedent, will most assuredly surrender), I've lost, and for good reason. No one picks a fight they think they can lose, and so overconfidence is your enemy, and a formidable one at that. Also avoid fights with men with scarring in a few telltale places: over/around the eyes and the ears. Noses are good to pay attention to but any idiot can get his nose broken. Men sporting cauliflower ears and scar tissue on their eyebrows only get that from training. And if he's training, he can probably kick your ass and at the very least will not hesitate a second to mix it up with you.

And not to get all Donahue on you, but if you don't have the moral imperative on your side, like say if, for example, you just burned him, fucked his old lady, or smashed into his car, you might want to let this one go because he's got at least three good reasons to kick your ass and you have, well, none actually.

SCENARIO SEGUNDO

Him: You talking to me?
You: No.
Him: You calling me a liar?
You: Well, no, I . . .
Him: I should FUCK you UP.

You: Hey, man, I . . .

Him: SHUT the fuck UP.

Now you should:

    A. SHUT the fuck UP?

    B. Keep alternating between "Well, no, I . . . " and "Hey, man, I . . . " until you eventually get hit.

    C. Leave as quickly as your scrawny legs will let you, Chicken Little. or

    D. Crack him in the mouth as soon as he says, "You calling me a liar?"

Answer Key

A. This works. Except it should be understood that fellows like this are just warming up and they don't intend to STOP the ritual humiliation until you are fellating them.

B. It is untrue that the longer he keeps up the questioning the less likely you are to get hit. You will get hit as soon as he gets bored, and with this Beaver Cleaver rapier-like repartee, that will, in all likelihood, be sooner rather than later.

C. Animals also love a fleeing target.

D. Why delay the inevitable? Take the fight to him and you might not have to take the fight much further. This is, win or lose, obviously the superior choice. Choose it and . . .

DON'T GO CRAZY

More fights are lost from the biophysical functioning of stress-induced fatigue than they are from inferior technique. In other words, relax. Like you would for a bicycle crash. Or a prostate exam. If you can fight with as much brio after five minutes (an eternity in fight time) as you can after twenty seconds, you will probably win. So realize time is on your side. While you need to fight with some sort of emotional content to your actions, anything too overboard will fuck you in the long run. I guarantee it.

Your best strike in this instance?

Well, since he's close enough to be having this conversation with you, go to the grappling card and use:

The Rear Naked Choke: Ducking under his left or right arm while staying close to his body, you take his back and wrap your right arm around his throat, grabbing your left shoulder. Now with your left hand, you bend it at the elbow,

DON'T MAKE THAT STUPID POST-FIGHT FACE

That fake smile guys do after they've had their ass kicked has got to go. It's the same face guys make when their girlfriend catches them cheating. It's the face of The Complete and Total Inability to Deal With the Fact That You Might Be Thought to Be a Pussy. And they always SAY the same thing with that fucking smile. They say, *"Did you see that?? The fucking guy sucker-punched me. What a bitch."* Then, four hours later you come back and you hear the guy going to some other poor bastard, *"Did you see that?? The fucking guy sucker-punched me. What a bitch."* Get over it. Or get the gun from your car and shoot the guy, but for God's sake don't keep this shit up.

putting your hand on the back of his hand and pushing it forward slightly while shrugging your shoulders. That's right. Easy for you, killer for him, and the best part of it is: you can talk to him the whole time.

DRAWBACKS: You could kill him and have a whole lot of *esplaining* to do, Lucy.

SCENARIO III:

Walking along the street, possibly lost in thought, you brush shoulders with someone. Looking up to apologize, you see him turning, stopping, and glowering. He then starts walking toward you. You:

- A. Finish your apology, throwing in a couple of gratuitous "Sirs" for good measure.
- B. Take two steps back for every one of his steps forward.
- C. Start singing your favorite Gilbert and Sullivan number.
  or
- D. Crack him in the mouth until he stops moving.

Answer Key

A. Only if you're in the army.

B. It's called the fucking tango. Enjoy it, Gertrude.

C. Called the Confusion Principle. It just might work.

D. Money move, baby! Money move!

HOPE FOR THE BEST, EXPECT THE WORST

Most humans who are not psychotic use a psychological technique called "ramping" immediately prior to conflict. Through a series of words, or "language structures," they get themselves warmed into the prospect of violent activity until, *voilà*, they've arrived at Fight Time. Get there before they do. And to paraphrase Motel 6's sage witness, Tom Bodette, "We'll remember to turn the lights off for you." Oh, by the way, I totally made up that psychology shit. Doesn't change the fact that if the dog is barking he's thinking about biting, though. Preferred technique in this instance?

The Uppercut: If someone is delivering a knockout punch, nine times out of ten it's the uppercut. Don't know whether it's the sharp clicking together of the jaw and the stimulation of some sort of nerve bundle but this punch is relatively easy to do and guaranteed to slip him into sleep. Throw your whole body into it and keep it tight against your body to start. Like a jack-in-the-box spring. And I ain't talking about the restaurant.

DRAWBACK: If your hand speed is slow, don't even THINK about trying this one.

And, finally, take strength from these last few indisputable facts:

A. Big guys usually don't know how to fight very well because they're used to using fear as a deterrent. Fight with these guys FIRST because even if you lose, people will think you're a stud, and who knows, you might actually WIN.

B. The first point's unspoken variant: don't assume that smaller guys are pushovers. Any ranked professional flyweight could brain-damage you into diapers.

C. Head butts work.

D. Do ANYTHING enough and you WILL get better at it. And, finally . . .

E. Choose friends you've seen fight before (and it's not whether they win or lose but whether or not they're even willing to go to the post) and make sure they've got your back. (You never know who's going to sit there holding the falafels while you get beaten with poolsticks.)

THE BEST FIGHT MOVIE OF ALL TIME ABOUT A NOW 85-YEAR-OLD MAN WHO COULD STILL KICK YOUR ASS

RAGING BULL (1980)
DIRECTED BY MARTIN SCORSESE

There are lots of reasons to love this movie but I'll start off with two. Two zen koan-like tales to burnish an already brilliant legacy of insanity, animal drive, and high culture craft.

Okay, here goes one: Back in the 1970s De Niro dated this woman who was friends with a friend of mine. They were all living down in SoHo before they were all rich and before SoHo had become the stomping ground for them and all the rest of New York's well-heeled. Anyways, this friend of mine was outraged and wouldn't be swayed by *Bang the Drum Slowly*, *Mean Streets*, or even the definitive New-York-that-no-longer-exists-1970s-movie *Taxi Driver*. De Niro was a piece of shit as far as she was concerned and it went on this way until finally I asked, "Why? I mean it sounds personal at this point?"

And she says, "Well, he used to go out with this friend of mine."

And I say, "So since when's that a crime?"

And she says, "Well, when she was dumping him, they were standing on the street corner and he slapped her on the ass."

"That sounds benign enough to me. I mean, a light slap on the ass, maybe in not the best of taste, but . . ."

"It knocked her *down*!"

I murmured apologias for a man I didn't even know, yet I had to secretly admit, to maybe no one but myself, that *that* was a money move. Purely because it delivered the unexpected and the untimely in a fashion that was decidedly unfashionable. It was a trifecta and it was like Bukowski said when defining style as "doing a dull or dangerous thing well." *And* it was politically incorrect during a time when political incorrectness was measured in grams.

And the second? A friend of my ex-agent and my ex-agent were chatting in a bar with this new "singer" who was being "managed" by her "manager" into a potentially, possibly "significant," "singing" "career" by none other than LaMotta. And while my ex-agent's friend talked to the ingénue, LaMotta fumed. Said nothing, but fumed. And my ex-agent's friend had a karaoke machine to sell her and, dammit, he would not be stopped. So they eventually come to some sort of accommodation and Jake finally pipes up, "You can go through me with that." And the ex-agent's friend pipes up gamely, "Oh, it's okay. It's light. I can just drop it off and . . . " And Jake freezes him with a look and says again, "You can go through me with that." And the conversation comes sliding down like a wall of wet sand. And when I ask the ex-agent if he got the sense that, given the situation, they might have stood a chance if it had come to blows, his answer was quick and definitive: "Fuck no." Golden years? You're god-damned right.

Get it? No?

Raging Bull is the greatest fight movie of all time, arguably the best Scorsese would ever make and De Niro would ever act in, and it flies off the screen like you were living it instead of watching it. And this shows: from Pesci's rib really getting broken in a sparring scene to De Niro really getting good enough with his pre-film prep to purportedly fight three fights out in Brooklyn, if you're a fan of the fistic arts, this is, colloquially, the SHIT. It's the truest to life in terms of how fighters fight in the ring and how they think when they think about how they fight in the ring.

Glorious and wrong all at the same time.

Yeah, you should be so lucky.

TWELVE

SO YOU'RE KNOCKED OUT:
OPTIONS TO CONSIDER

THE THRILL OF UNDEFEAT, OR, ONE MAN'S PEEK INTO THE YAWNING MAW OF TOTAL PERSONAL FAILURE AND ITS TRANSCENDENCE MEASURED OUT ONE FIGHT AT A TIME. LADIES AND GENTLEMEN: GILBERT MELENDEZ

It's a rarefied club. If you're a real fighter who fights real fights, it's a club you'll eventually probably be knocked the fuck out of. That being: The Undefeated. And so it is that any fighter who is undefeated after ten fights is either fighting worked matches (a.k.a. fixed fights) or is a true phenom.

Gilbert Melendez is this phenom. A mixed martial arts phenom. A 10-0 phenom, though, given the frequency with which he fights, that could radically have changed by the time you read this. But that's almost immaterial to everybody else, or at least the everybody else who knows that beating ten men, shit, forget about men, ten professional fighters, in a row, seven by KO or TKO, one by submission, and two by decisions, is the kind of thing everybody else would gladly say is good enough. Everybody, that is, *except* him.

What makes Sammy run?

"I go out to kill."

And for this to have any weight at all you have to hear him say it when you can see him say it. The first time I saw Melendez fight was only the second time he had fought. It was March 27, 2003, and he had just come back from spring break. He was wearing surf jams. And smiling as he walked into the caged ring. He was 5'9" and 155 pounds. He reminded me of a muppet. My pre-fight prediction was that he was going to lose. Badly.

Except he did not.

He won. Badly. His opponent, one Mr. Jeff Hougland, virtually disappeared under a hail of blows. And after the ref stood him from where he had been delivering aforementioned bombs to the face of Mr. Hougland, he was smiling again.

So the whole "killing" thing seems out of character. Until you start to track his whole march uphill. One win after the next. Here in the States. In Japan. And with each step you can feel something working its way through.

"Well, I can't deny that I think about it now. I'm thinking 'no way can I lose now.' That's what I'm thinking about when I train. I'm also thinking of how much I hate whoever it is I'm fighting."

And the smile again.

At twenty-four, Melendez is training in San Luis Obispo with one of the world's premier fighters, Chuck Liddell, a fellow traveler. Liddell, who had been looking at the same sort of future that Larry Holmes saw—always winning but never getting any respect for doing so—before he drove home in the most definitive way possible that he didn't care whose body he had to walk over to get to where he is now, is arguably one of the best two or three fighters in the world at his weight class. And his quiet desire to crush, kill, and destroy matches Melendez's quite well.

"You want to know what I do before the fights that I win? I have Jake Shields [a world champion] hit me in the face. I stay in my little room backstage. I like to keep it like a jail cell. Shut up or get the fuck out. I cage my beast inside and try to turn my nervousness into energy. I listen to some music . . . "

Classical?

"Haha . . . no. Some rap. Or some Rage Against the Machine."

And gone is his smile of old. In fact, he no longer smiles at all when he enters the ring, instead preferring to run into the ring, his eyes like the backs of matchbooks, all gray and shark-like, over a mouth that silently mutters what I imagine are the kind of words you whisper to God about something you really, really want.

"I want to kill whoever it is I'm fighting." And in front of 25,000 people at the Tokyo Dome, or in front of 14,000 in San Jose, this has been made aggressively apparent. Time after time after time after time after time (and now double that). With his father in his corner (so the whole Freudian thing is shot to hell right there), Melendez does exactly that.

And losing is not really an issue at the same time that it is really the *only* issue, but this kind of hunger is a bitch, and whatever it is about Melendez that makes winning such a tonic for whatever it is that might ail him, we can only imagine that he hates losing much more than he loves winning. Which, as of this writing, he was still doing.

Well, that and riding limos to shows, dating models, and beating the crap out of larger men on the street just because they don't know any better.

Welcome to the hall of champions, goddamnit.

MODERN CINEMA'S LONGEST CONTINUOUS SINGLE-SHOT FIGHT SCENE STARRING A MAN WHO MADE HIS LIVING IN A KILT AND THE BLACK MICHAEL CAINE, KEITH DAVID

THEY LIVE (1988) DIRECTED BY JOHN CARPENTER

Screen time is alternate reality time. If the average conversation seems interminable when you're talking about someone else's dreams, or *Star Trek* or something else you give not the slightest shit about, ON screen it would seem like a lifetime. Or a Lars Von Trier film. But nowhere is this LESS true than in the parallel universe of screen fight scenes.

Flash to: waiting at some dusty California train yard. Two railroad workers are angrily jawing in the front seat of a pickup truck. They exit their respective doors like the truck was on fire and begin throwing off various articles of clothing in the world's oldest pre-fight ritual of ramping. Also known as getting up the nerve. The words rumble across the parking lot, and when they've both thrown off the gloves, the hard hats, the vests, and the shirts they have absolutely no other option but to start swinging.

And they do.

Swinging, missing, slowing, and then the harsh reality: the average person cannot even swing their arms vigorously for sixty seconds, let alone hit another human being, without doing what we in the biz like to call GASSING. Which they do. The fight having ended inconclusively, the two begin redressing with the shirt, the vests, the hard hats, and the gloves before, like some weird kinescope that's been run in reverse, they're sitting in the front seat of the pickup truck, only this time, they're completely silent.

Total elapsed time: one minute and seventeen seconds.

Which is why this movie, *They Live*, starring former "professional" "wrestler" Rowdy Roddy Piper, is sooooo goddamned unusual. Sure there was the rolling and rollicking fight scene between John Wayne and Victor McLaglen in John Ford's 1952 flick *The Quiet Man*, but this occurs over changes in scenario and therefore falls out of consideration in this here category.

Over a great potboiling theme of aliens disguised as humans that are revealed through the use of special glasses in a scene that features the non-kilted Mr. Piper trying to convince the hardest-working black man in Hollywood, Keith David, that the aliens DO exist, they begin an alley fight that while it was only meant to last twenty seconds in the original script, clocked in at an amazing five minutes and twenty seconds of screen time.

Add to that the fact that "method actors" Piper and David decided to fight for real, only faking face punches, and it emerges as a stunningly Proustian bit of filmmaking, and for this, and his total lack of interest in the governorship of Minnesota, we give a tip of the hat to The Rowdy One.

EDDIE'S DEAD. LONG LIVE EDDIE.

This was a head shot. Plain and simple. Because you could talk to the next ten fight gamers you meet and not get the same kind of unapologetic depth that you get when you get an Eddie Goldman. And every sport's got an Eddie Goldman: bodybuilding had Ricky Wayne, baseball had Billy Martin, tennis had McEnroe. Guys that are—if not honor-bound to do so are then constitutionally incapable of NOT doing so—going to give you the straight shot and fuck you if you don't like it.

Right or wrong, lucid or snockered, their unfettered opinionating usually marks them as guys that either have to make their mark where they can't be touched—on some field of play—or they get hustled off, stage right, to make room for more accommodating (read: bought) voices. *Or* they die in fiery car wrecks with a bottle of Smirnoff clutched to their chests.

In any case, with Goldman, thus far, feel free to check none of the above (www.secondsout.com/radio/).

He also, thus far, has managed to, wait, let's put that between quotes . . . "has managed to" stay out of any significant amounts of limelight despite being knee deep in almost every fight game there is—amateur wrestling, real pro wrestling, fake pro wrestling, real fake pro wrestling, ultimate fighting, kickbox-ing, boxing, real, fake, fixed, and otherwise. And his Rolodex of people he's

touched just goes on and on and on. Despite his dyspepsia. Despite his continued lack of interest in the vicissitudes of the business world that guides sports—in particular, fight sports—and finally, despite every single prevailing trend there is that's connected to sports entertainment, Goldman perseveres, jeremiads and all. When I ask him, after finally getting hold of him, if there are any sports untainted by the bony hand of avarice, he says without missing a beat:

"No."

Which is why he had to be tracked down. Like that cereal Life that was foisted on the Madison Ave.–manufactured Mikey back in the '70s on the grounds that because he hated everything, if he LIKED the cereal it had to have something going for it, Goldman could be counted on to deliver nothing but: head shots, that is.

You've got a history that goes back in the fight game forever it seems, fading in and out according to your whims, focusing on this fight sport or that. Did you have a Pearl Harbor moment when you came out of the cold this last time? For me it was in the early '90s when I saw the first UFC.

I missed the first UFC. I later saw it but I missed the first one. But my Pearl Harbor moment was when I was reading about extreme fighting, whose press conference I had been to early on in the year, at Kahnawake, the Mohawk Nation near Montreal. And there's been a whole history of political struggles there and the government didn't want them there and I'm sitting around in my apartment with the TV on, thinking "What the hell am I doing sitting here? I got to get myself up there," and that really sort of marked a turnaround because I had already started covering this a bit. That, of course, was the event where eight participants—Ralph Gracie, Zinoviev, and so on—were arrested, which led to this whole huge struggle, and it ended up getting an article in *Penthouse* because of that . . . but what was important, what was gotten across, was the pleas by the members of the Mohawk Nation for their people to fight against genocide and for self-determination. For their rights as a people.

And that to me was the centerpiece of the whole issue and that's why that whole thing was so important beyond just the battle to legalize mixed martial arts, because it wasn't even known as that then, and the whole promoting of combat sports . . .

So was the upshot, then, that fight sports and social activism lived happily ever after?

The upshot was that most of the charges were thrown out, and a lot of the people saw that it was absurd that these people were arrested. . . . I think one fighter had

to pay a fine or something like that. The prison that they were thrown in was shortly thereafter closed down because it was found to be inhumane. . . . I mean, look, Canadians, who don't have as much of a cowboy attitude about these things as Americans do, were asking "What? We're arresting people because they're going to a live sporting event? That was open to the public and was shown on television? What's going on here? You don't like it? You don't have to watch it. You didn't have to fight in it. You didn't have to go there. What's the big deal?"

So in '96 there was a whole battle and eventually it got legalized but this was part of a whole broader struggle that was going on between the Canadian and Quebec governments against the native people in Canada. But this turned around and rules were adopted for no-holds-barred fighting, which were then adopted, in most cases, in California in 2000, which lead to New Jersey adopting them, then Nevada unified the rules, which opened the whole door up.

But this door-opening thing is not to your liking, it seems. You've told me you won't even watch the UFC anymore. Is it because it failed on some sort of social-relevance scale?
All you have to do is go back to the 1919 Black Sox scandal. Back then there were three major sports in America: baseball, boxing, and wrestling. Now, all of these sports faced crises of their own and all went in different directions as a result of it. Baseball had the fixing of the 1919 World Series. In response they brought in a commissioner and outlawed gambling, and they laid down the law.

Boxing had been illegal in many places so what they did then was legalize it. But instead of creating a league or a commissioner or something like that, it was regulated by the state commissions.

Professional wrestling had this problem of real and fake matches, and look, the problem with a lot of these matches back then was that the fans found them dissatisfying *because* they were real; they usually lasted a really long time, and were slow on the action. Promoters said, 'We'll make it more entertaining by making it fake.' And they did this more and more up until the late 1980s, when they dropped any pretense that it was real.

So these were three different routes taken for combat sports, actually all sports in general. But boxing, under the state commissions, was able to legalize itself without having a central body, but this eventually has led to its downfall: now you have multiple champions. It's the only sport where you don't have a single champion. Not having a central body has really hurt boxing. You don't have the best guys fighting the best guys, you have these sanctioning bodies pushing mandatory fights, multiple titles, and utter confusion. You know what question I get a lot? 'Who's the heavyweight champion today?' And when you try to explain . . . the WBA, the IBF, and WBC and WBO and guys from the Ukraine, and guys from Belorussia, and Kazakhstan, and St. Petersburg— Russia, not Florida—it just gets very, very confusing. No unified titles. No central governing body.

And here's something: the networks in particular don't want it. Because it'd be very hard for them to control one guy. Most of the promoters don't want it either, except for, ironically, Don King. Now, he has contracts with a lot of these guys either promoting or co-promoting a number of these different guys.

So Don King's interested in a central body?

No. NONE of these guys are interested in a central body. King's interested in unifying the titles. There was a proposal a few years ago put forth by boxing promoter Lou DiBella to hold a meeting among different boxing promoters and none of the other major promoters even wanted to HOLD A MEETING together. It's very self-destructive. But there's hope for boxing because it's still the most polished and professional of the combat sports on the top level. The skill you see among the top fighters when you have top people matched up against each other, in terms of punching, is unmatched. And many people in mixed martial arts recognize this. [MMA champ] Frank Shamrock said the same thing. The striking, very often, in mixed martial arts sucks. The striking sucks and these guys have no chins.

Is that why [HBO and NBC sports commentator] Jim Lampley hates it?

Well, I don't want to put words in his mouth, but he doesn't approve of it and he doesn't like it. I don't think he understands grappling and I think as a boxing guy he's appalled at the use of strikes that are not legal in boxing. Not only dirty boxing, like holding and hitting, but knees and elbows, and he doesn't understand grappling, and so when it goes to the ground and takedowns and submission moves . . . look, it's, for him, probably like when an ugly American starts making fun of someone Chinese by talking faux Chinese or something. It just seems kind of insulting. I've tried to goad him on when I talk with him about it, because he IS a big supporter of wrestling at the Olympics, but he just didn't get it.

Well the early-stage knock against it had very much to do with this idea that fighting for the sake of fighting was somehow irredeemable. That if you removed the mask that's provided when you add a ball or a stick or something and just had two men going at it, well it was, to quote John McCain, "Human cockfighting."

Let me just make clear that though I follow the business aspects because it's important, and the media aspects, I take a broader view. To me whether something is socially positive and useful and desirable is not based on the ratings that it gets. It could be totally the opposite. Or it could be totally the same. It could be important from a business perspective for the media to follow the ratings and so on, and so I report on these things, but when I see what a group like IFL [International Fight League] is doing by emphasizing SPORTSMANSHIP in MMA versus what the UFC [Ultimate Fighting Championship] is doing, which is emphasizing stupidity and trash talking and all kinds of negative values, well I . . . Look, I don't care that all of the music today emphasizes negative values. I look at things broader historically, and not according to some MTV short-attention-span clock. There's a real softness, a real parasitic attitude of enjoying having people doing everything else for you, and yeah, a fixation on negative values. The US government is afraid of having a draft for their failed war in Iraq that's even more unpopular, I guess, than Vietnam was, but nobody's saying anything because there's no draft. So we rely on air power, which never works, and this was the Rumsfeld strategy and he should have known better. I mean this is a guy who was a wrestler.

So was Jesse "The Body" Ventura.

Well, Rumsfeld was a wrestler at Princeton, I think he was captain of his team and then later he won some kind of Navy championship, but he became this corporate guy who was serving these corporate interests and his intelligence got trumped by all of this stuff. And he was, to his credit, though I'd never vote for him or his people, instrumental when the liberal types were trying to get rid of wrestling at Princeton. He and the alumni got together to get wrestling back. But my point is that even outside of the business, fighting or sports can have a tremendously positive effect upon you.

How?

"It builds self-confidence, it shows you the connection between mental and physical fitness, it'll give you an attitude of struggling for your rights, it'll show that you're not someone who's going to be pushed around, it'll teach you when to fight, how to fight. That was [Nelson] Mandela's point about it. He was an amateur boxer and he credited that for teaching him strategy and tactics. He wasn't a fan of the violence, but that was part of it, and when you're involved in political struggles and revolutionary wars, you're not a fan of violence but you realize it's necessary.

By any means necessary and *No holds barred* are very similar slogans, and that's not a coincidence. A lot of this is not new, but particularly in our parasitic age . . . we have a so-called financial-services industry that's huge and that creates nothing of value. . . . You have a lot of people who are parasites. Particularly in one of the richest countries in the world, but not only. But this is something that goes against that and relates more to the culture of the working-class people. People who still have to work for a living, whether it's a physical job or service, or retail, or whatever.

But traditionally combat "sports" have always been the purview of the upper classes: think dueling and fencing and so on.

Well . . . yeah, you had Aaron Burr and Alexander Hamilton, but it existed on different levels. If you've ever read any of Frederick Douglass's writings he talks about how boxing and wrestling were really popular among the slaves. Between Christmas and New Year's and so on when the slave owners were drunk and so on, the slaves would have competitions in their time off. So it was popular on all levels. But I don't make fighting an abstract ideal. You do it because you HAVE to. It is a practical necessity. Fighting to live, for most people, is a practical necessity. And sports combat is just the way to teach you how to do that for whatever kind of battle you're in.

But to play devil's advocate here a minute, isn't that supposed to be one of the values of civilization? That we create social structures so that we DON'T have to fight to live? We create social structures today, and the ones that dominate are all designed to confuse the majority of people into making a minority of the people rich and powerful. And dividing them up to get them to kill each other on the behalf of various ruling groups. This [fight training] helps build an attitude of defiance as well to conventional thinking. Or it can.

But I'm an elitist at base level and start to think that when you talk about wanting to free the common man, it's an incomplete discussion if you're not also talking about *advancing* the common man. Which nobody is. And so whose fault is it if we're stupid? "It's all *supposed* to be dumbed down, though. That's the whole point. In the early days of the UFC, for example, it was an incredible atmosphere. It was like the United Nations at these events. Fighters and fight fans from Brazil and Japan and from Europe sharing techniques and this and that. It was an incredible thing. And it was the same thing when I went to Brazil or Japan. Now they put a few people on a reality TV show and they say, "Uhhh . . . I wanna mess him up, man . . . uhhhh . . ." And some people might say this makes it successful, but I don't. I don't think it's highly successful. I know it has good ratings and good buy rates. To me it's socially not successful.

Look, is the WWE [World Wrestling Entertainment] successful for combat sports?

They draw more people than the UFC does. They did better than that. They're a publicly traded company. They make a ton of money. Is that more successful? That's not the issue. What are they promoting? They're not promoting honor. They're not promoting something that you could point out to people as something that will improve you as people. And particularly a people that are disenfranchised, that are out of control and that need a warrior culture to help them battle for their rights and livelihood. Not this. This has been remade in the image of their—the gambling casino owners' and their ex-boxercise instructor's—gods.

Yes, sports IS entertainment and it has to have entertainment value. If it doesn't have entertainment value, people won't pay money to go watch it. But there's a social value to it as well that I'm more concerned with; that for me trumps everything. In other words, I'm not a capitalist. I'm not *interested* in maximizing profits and the accumulation of capital. That's what they're interested in and that trumps everything else for them and that's the direction that's led it, especially in the culture we have today, to the lowest common denominator. Especially with a network like SpikeTV.

I don't know that what you're even asking for is possible. Something with a high social value, high financial value? And is entertaining? What does that even look like?

Look at Muhammad Ali's career. That was key to him being viewed as the most popular and most important professional athlete in the twentieth century. Maybe the best-known person in the whole world. For his struggle—even though he was misguided into the Nation of Islam—against racism, white supremacy, the Vietnam War. All of these things added in to the whole allure of Muhammad Ali.

But intra-sport controversy concerning his legitimacy surrounded even him from the beginning. Did you read Nick Tosches's book on Sonny Liston and the bit on the so-called phantom punch that led to the defeat that made Ali's bones?

I didn't read it. And I don't know how much that was based on fact . . . because I remember trying to interview him [Tosches] on it and he wasn't interested in talking about it and so I've spoken to people who knew what he wrote and were involved at the time and they said that he really didn't know a lot about what he was talking about. Now people have different opinions about

whether or not those first fights with Ali and Liston were fixed or not. But that to me, even if they were true, doesn't stain his legacy at all, because what did he do after that?

Well, I've chatted with Howard Bingham [noted Ali photographer], as well as a former sparring partner of Liston's and gotten two highly entrenched, but persuasive positions on either side.

I've heard both sides of the argument too. In a fixed fight it doesn't mean you aren't going to get punched. You know the other guy's going to be throwing punches, so if you want to fix the fight you get hit and you go down and you stay down. But . . . I don't know enough. I do know that even if it was fixed it doesn't change his legacy because not all the fights were fixed. But . . . you know, we're in a period of cynicism. Look what people have done with freedom? Hip-hop music that calls each other the names that are used now.

Is there any sport that's a standard bearer for our higher yearnings, then?
No.

And that's not cynical? What about baseball?!?

I can't watch baseball anymore. Not because it's slow but because it's corrupt. I'm not going to pay a bunch of money to watch a bunch of steroid guys play. From 1957 to like 1993 I used to go to baseball games all the time, every year. And then one game I noticed that they had Steve Howe pitching and I knew he already had been busted six or seven times for drugs and I'm asking, "Why am I watching this?" I didn't go back.

But for combat sports, for all these sports I'm not saying there's no hope. I'm just saying it's an uphill battle, but anything decent in society usually is. That doesn't mean you stop struggling, or fighting. It just means you want to start to lay out lessons from this retrograde, regressive period we're in. I mean, who knows when things will start to turn around? I'm never without hope. I think we should just be more focused on making a contribution that's lasting, that's all.

THIRTEEN

"I KILLED A MAN"

Some of the following names and places have been changed to protect the innocent and/or those likely to be prosecuted.

You learn at a certain point to pay attention to nuance, like when you hear a voice on the phone that sounds a little too eager, or in this case morose. It was a guy whom I trained: a thirty-something-hipster who dug the fight game first as a spectator and then, drawn along by temperament, as a practitioner. He had bought a couple of mats and spread them all across his ten-by-ten-foot second-floor apartment and a couple of times a week we'd roll . . . through the basics, some catch wrestling arcana, some refinements of the Brazilian jiu-jitsu he had started to study . . . before we'd just go at it: smashing into the walls, jammed up against the couch, or off mat onto his uncarpeted floor. His unspoken goal, like any good student, was to ultimately kick my ass—an attempt I wholeheartedly supported him trying since his rabid desire for comeuppance fueled my equally rabid desire to never be bested by someone who knew what the hell I knew *well* after I knew it.

But there was this call. His girlfriend had trained too, wisely not with me, though, and had even scored a W by choke at a company Christmas party over an over-lubed boss who after he had found out that she studied begged her to "come on . . . show me what you got." At 5'5" she most certainly did and he found himself waking up more than once that day; this time off of someone's floor.

So I figured the call had everything to do with, you know, the perils of Pauline and the rocky path of young love and what not. And I chuckled at, inadvisably, anyone asking *me* for relationship advice. I chuckled, sipped some tea, and read with great interest an item in the local paper that detailed a street scuffle that had turned violent.

The story was pitched as a sideline to the continuing drumbeat of a story that you seem to read in weeklies all over America about gentrification, also known as: what happens when poor folks live alongside not-so-poor folks who, drawn by the neighborhood's "color," move in and start driving rents up. That's the public story.

The real story is that there are enough poor folk around, of very many colors, to populate a lot of these neighborhoods a few times over, and so it goes, the lost tribes of near-broke post-college types back to back with resentful locals. An uneasy peace seems to exist, except, as the paper tells it, this one night it didn't, and a local who had, on the occasion of his fortieth birthday, pulled his car up to the curb a few blocks from his home in a general mood to party, sat carside and played his car radio as loud as it seemed like his car radio could be played. At 1:30 in the morning.

And at this point in the story I started to curse the decline in American mores and manners. I decried the miserable me-firstist get-over-itis that infects even our most mundane interactions. As I read on, I found myself desiring some sort of just resolution to what appeared to be unchecked assholism. And it arrived in the form of a nearby apartment resident who appeared on the scene and in the ensuing request to turn down said music got into a fight that ended up leaving the offender dead. I turned the page, finished breakfast, and moved on.

Next week or so I go to my young charge's house for some training and he's not much in the mood, and he and his girl are exchanging quick looks and in a blurt he tells me what you've already guessed at this point: it was him.

Fill in the details for me. I mean, did the papers get it right?

Yeah, basically. I was sleeping at the time—1:30 in the morning. I sleep in a loft and so I had to get out of the loft, put my clothes on, go downstairs, prop the outside door open, and go outside. I'm pretty easygoing. You know, I'm not a hard-on or nothing like that. I don't get into fights usually. But he had played about three full songs on the radio. You know how when you're sitting in your car and you can feel the guy's music in another car? *Boom boom boom boom*? It was like that. Only closer. It was right under my window. I later found out it was his fortieth birthday and he had gone out and whooped it up. He had cocaine on him, was having a good time, and I got nothing against someone having a good time. He was just coming home. I think he was sobering up or something. The windows were all down so he probably drove there trying to sober up. It was a cold night. It was February 5, 2003.

Shouting "shut the fuck up" out of your window? Not an option?
You know what? The first thing I did was go to my refrigerator and pulled out some eggs. I went back to the window, looked out at his car and I was going to throw the fucking egg but I said to myself, You know what? That's only going to escalate the situation. He's drunk or whatever. He's in his car. Some beater. And then I finally figured: he knows where I live, this is ridiculous, right out of your own window. So I put the eggs down and I go downstairs. My girlfriend's awake now and she's giving me a hard time about how loud the guy is. You know, there had been times before when this happened and she went down and I had to follow to keep her from kicking somebody's ass. She's this tiny thing but she's tough. So I figure this time I'm going to go out because it's better because I'm the cooler head. I'm Mr. Nice Guy. I mean, I never get into fights.

Except for that picture I've seen of you fighting those guys at the Dirty Three show.
Hey, man, that wasn't my fault. These assholes were getting kind of surly with the woman I was there with when they asked everybody to sit and they refused to and she couldn't see from where she was sitting behind them. So I got into a fight with these two guys. I mean, what is it? I'm like a magnet for assholes. Anyways, I go down, I got slippers on, for chrissakes. Just pants, no underwear. No shirt, even. Now I can see him. He's looking kind of dozy. This makes me not nervous. I'm thinking to myself, All right. I've dealt with alcoholics before. And they can act violent but usually they're pretty dopey. They don't usually start throwing punches, and if they do they're really wobbly and it's not hard to contain them. So I ask him to turn his radio down but I'm having to pantomime and scream because he can't hear anything, but I'm making the motion like, Hey! C'mon. Gimme a break. Turn it down. Now instead of just turning it down he opens up his door and starts moving around the back of the car. I walk, simulta-

neously past him toward his now-open car door. I'm in the street and his car was parked. He follows me back to where I'm standing by his car door.

Did you look at him as you passed each other?
I don't remember. I just thought he was a drunk so I wasn't really paying attention. But he's now screaming at me to not touch his radio and now I'm not cool anymore, really. I've lost my cool. I'm screaming at him now because he didn't just turn the fucking radio down. But I'm nervous about getting into his car. I feel like I want to just reach over and turn the damn thing off. Grab his keys, something. The guy shouldn't be driving anyway. But I don't want to turn my back to him. So I'm yelling at him, he keeps coming closer, we keep yelling at each other, and out of nowhere—and I really didn't see it and I think I'm pretty savvy about things but he was pretty fast—he comes up with a left hook and hit me in the temple with his keys in his fist. Now, I didn't see his fist so I didn't know what he had in his fist, all I know now is that my head's bleeding and I didn't know this but head wounds bleed *profusely*. So it was flooding. Flooding over my eyes. It freaked the shit out of me because I thought I was being stabbed. And he hit me multiple times. Maybe a half a dozen times. So I close the gap, get a bear hug and tackle him by hooking my foot behind his leg. He was a lot stronger than I thought he was going to be, for one thing, but I thought he was just going to be a drunk but maybe he was a little amped up on the coke. We were about the same weight and height but I get him to the ground, I pass his guard [a Brazilian jiu-jitsu maneuver whereby you escape from the encircling legs of a downed opponent], sit on his stomach, and just start teeing off on him. Probably about the same amount of times as he hit me. Then he rolled over on his stomach, giving me his back, and I held him until the police got there.

So you put in the choke.
[Silence]

Okay. So what happens when the police get there?
Well, the whole thing took about three minutes. It seemed like an eternity but I'm pretty sure that if we had wanted to, we could have probably held our breath through the whole thing. But I held him down and another guy from a car that had pulled up is helping me hold him down and the cops show up not thirty seconds after that. People had called the police. I was yelling for people to call the police. And there were tons of witnesses at this point. All the neighbors and so

on. The police come, I step up off the guy and I'm thinking, Arrest that man, you know what I mean? He just fucking assaulted me. There was no excuse. When I came out I didn't even come out yelling at him. But then I see the police pull a yellow sheet over him and I'm thinking this doesn't look good.

What did you see when you stepped off of him?
He started shaking and he spits up blood. Blood came out of his mouth, like about eight inches. A stream of it. A spurt. I could see it from twenty feet away, which is where they had hustled me to after they came. And I thought, Good. Now that fool can go to jail. Then, I stopped paying attention to him but next thing I know they were putting a yellow plastic sheet over him. That doesn't seem like what you take a person to the hospital in, is what I thought to myself. I was pretty fucking freaked out at this point. The police were relatively cool. I mean they got kind of a gallows humor, and all the way to the station I got called "tough guy" and "bruiser'" and stuff like that. I'm like, "Dude, the mother-fucker's dead . . . c'mon. You gotta have some respect for something." On the other hand they were pretty sympathetic and they said, "You got it bad, man, because anybody would have done what you did. You just defended yourself."

But they took me downtown. It was so early that the detectives were still asleep. I had to wait in a holding cell there and I was like show-and-tell for the cops. I got a bandage on my head, blood all over. And the cops would bring guys through and it'd be like, "You see what happens? This guy was now just minding his own business and now some fool is dead!" And guys in there are looking and me and asking, "Hey, man? You know some kung fu shit?" I'm getting big respect in this little holding cell with these penny-ante criminals—guys who steal bikes and shit like that for their crack habit. And the cops are trying to turn it into some kind of cautionary tale. Which, of course it should be, but nobody in there was about to start paying attention to any cops. Most of them were in there for stupid shit, but some of them had been in there because they had gotten into fights. And so the cops were like, "Look. This is what can happen." I mean, most people, who get into fights, the first thing they think is "What's the worst that can happen to *me*?" Well, what if the opposite happens? What, if you punch this fool . . .

Look, I read about a guy who that happened to because the same time that this happened to me I was hyperaware of these stories in the paper. But this kid in high school gets into this fight in the parking lot. Just kids getting into a fight. He hit the guy ONE TIME. The other guy falls back and hits his head on the bumper thing that the car parks against? Dead. One punch. And people want to file murder charges against this guy. I'm thinking, Murder? Who is thinking these kinds of things? At best he was thinking he wanted to push the guy's nose in or something.

So was it like a cop show after that? A single bulb in a room with an extremely shaky camera or something?

It *was* kind of like a cop show. Two detectives. But the photographer came in first and started snapping pictures. Two or three rolls of footage. All sides, bruises and cuts. I still have a scar across my back from the keys. They went pretty deep. He wasn't holding back. Neither one of us were holding back. But the detectives asked me, "How hard did you hit him?" As hard as I could. Turns out that was the right answer. The honest answer was the right answer. The fact that I had been training turned out to my advantage also. I had no police record and I had been training and so the detective was saying that if an ordinary person . . . I mean, the amount of damage that happened to this guy was not consistent with how it'd play out with a normal person. I trained, so of course he was going to get hurt worse than he would with some guy who does nothing.

So they take the pictures. Then what happens?

A lot of nerves for like two years. I have to give blood, they swab your mouth, test under your fingernails, your mucus membranes. But I talk to them until about eight in the morning and I got to make a phone call and I found out later that the phone I was talking on was not tapped but I was being videotaped as I talked. And the room was being tapped and I was being monitored. But you know my feeling on all of this is that it *is* a cautionary tale. I've read your writing before, I know your whole bit about how it's better to take your lumps and get your ass kicked standing up for yourself than to have to walk away and feel the shame of that for the rest of your life. And I had always agreed with that. Now? I have a different take. Now I feel that, and I don't want to make myself too heroic in this whole thing, but I feel like the Duke in *The Quiet Man*. That's how I feel.

I don't want to fight. Now I'd like to start training a little bit again, but for a long time I saw violence everywhere. I couldn't watch *The Simpsons* without cringing at Homer throttling Bart. Even people yelling at each other on the street about minor parking things . . . I think everybody's too sensitive about stuff. Somebody cuts you off in traffic, or cuts in front of you in line? Shit, man, these are perceived slights. Have a little largesse and stop being petty motherfuckers who look for this shit. Because what if you do some shit and the guy dies? And *then* what?

Then you have to go to court and see the guy's daughter in a puddle of tears. I had to sit across from her, and she's bawling, you know? She was about eighteen. And his son was about sixteen. They were estranged and he had kind of abandoned them, but he was trying to reconcile. He was a chef, too. I learned that his family were good people. He had had problems. Alcohol and drug problems but he was trying to work them out. He had violence problems, issues in the past, starting fights in bars and so on. He was working on himself and went out and whooped it up and he got into a fight that he shouldn't have. He'd probably gotten into plenty of fights before but never came out of any of them dead. You only do that once.

What happened with the court case?

This was civil court. Criminal charges were never filed because the DA's office found that were no grounds to do so. It was mutual combat, or mutual combatants, or something like that, but that didn't go anywhere. But he died of multiple traumatic injuries, the coroner decided, and so the family went after me for wrongful death, but it was also dismissed. The criminal case is always open, I guess, until they bring charges, but as far as I know we're done.

So now that you have this whole Kwai Chang Caine thing going on, how's it been going being this minister of peace?

Well, I've had four incidents since then. One happened a little bit after this whole thing was over. My girlfriend and I were riding our bikes up the street. We're going to see a movie and it was a sketchy neighborhood so I should have known or suspected. But down in the distance we see this couple at a cab and it's like she's going to jump in the car and he's goofing with her. It's like they're teasing each other. But as we get closer we can see that she's trying to get away from this guy. She's kicking at him and he's going into the back of the cab and he's trying to hit her and stuff. The cabdriver's doing nothing. He's scared shitless. I'm now at the front, near the driver's side and I hit the hood with my hand and I hold up my phone. You see, the phone is the thing. So I hold up my phone and say, "Do I have to call the police?" That's what people need to know, that the phone is the thing. Just pull out your phone. "Do I gotta call the police? I mean I can do that while I run away from you." So he pops his head out of the car, lets go of her, and the car drives off but now he's up in my grill and he's pissed. And this is two weeks after the other thing and my girlfriend is now scared to death. The guy starts talking about how it was all the girl's fault. I mean, I'm a nice guy and so if he's willing to talk I'm okay. And it was over in two seconds. I just told him, "Look, you don't want the kind of trouble I just had. You wanna hit somebody, you do it in the privacy of your house because the reality of it is you can't hit somebody in public without the public getting involved. But if you're standing out in the street and you're hitting somebody? I'm going to call the police." And he just walked off.

The next one was at a café. This girl sees these guys out of the corner of her eye as she sits at this café. She feels bad. She feels guilty because she's white, they're black, and so she doesn't want to put her purse away because it'll seem like she doesn't trust them. But these guys were sketchy as fuck. I mean, if you see a white guy all tatted up with prison tattoos you're right to maybe not trust him. Your spidey sense was tingling and you ignore it, so I don't feel sorry for these girls at all. But I find this all out later. Apparently she had her purse out and these guys snatched it off of the back of the chair. So now I'm walking down the street and I hear "Stop, stop! Those guys got my purse!!!" Then I see these two guys running in the bike lane and these two girls chasing them. Now they take off across the street and, hey, I'M not going to get involved. I mean, I got my own problems. I'm not going to be a superhero. Honestly, I did not want to get involved in this, BUT . . . the fool ran right back across the street, right in front of me, and about three yards in front of me he's dumping stuff out of the purse and stuffing the money into his pockets.

But this time I'm right on top of him and so I grabbed him and I just say, "Gimme the money." So now his friend comes over and his friend is a foot taller than me but I still got the first guy and so I grab the second guy by the wrist so I can control him and I'm just trying to explain to these guys that I don't want any trouble but I'm thinking to myself, "How do I get into this kind of shit?"

So the guy starts in with, "We didn't do nothing" and I say, "'Hey, I'm not the police, man. I got nothing to argue about here, I just want the money. I WANT the money. Give it to me. There's no judge or jury here. We're not going to trial. I just want the money. Either that or these girls are going to call the police and I guarantee you I can hold on to you, at least one of you, until the cops get here."

Of course, they gave up all the money and they walk off and the girls told me all of what happened and I was thinking, Dude, if I had known that you were so stupid, I would not even have stepped into this.

The last two were at a nightclub in Oakland where me and my new girlfriend went dancing. Two altercations in one night. At the same place. We were having a good time and we threw our coats and things on this pile. So we decide we're going to go out and have a cigarette and so we grab our stuff and some guy comes up to me and accuses me of taking his girlfriend's purse. Now, my girl is in the bathroom and this guy's facing me outside the bathroom, trying to get the purse from me. So he says, "Yo, you took my girlfriend's purse." And so I tell him, "I don't see any girlfriend."

This is going on for a minute or two with him telling me how he's going to kick my ass and I tell him he's going to HAVE to kick my ass to get this purse because I'm not going to let him steal the purse of the girl I'm with.

Now, this is not a bad guy, right? It's just some guy who is trying to get hold of a purse that he thinks belongs to his old lady, right?
Turns out it is. Fuck. Let's just say I was buying drinks later and he was very cool about the whole thing because his girlfriend comes out of the bathroom, I ask her to open it and show me it's hers, and it's hers, and at this point my girl has come out and says, "That's not my purse." I had no idea. And I was telling the guy shit like, "You know, if you even HAVE a girlfriend, which I am having a hard time believing . . . well, IF she comes out, we'll see." And I'm talking to the guy like this while the guy is up in my grill telling me he's going to kick my ass.

But afterward we're making friends, right? We're laughing about it actually and I lean back and knock some guy's drink over on top of one of those tabletop video-game things. So I say, "Dude, I'm sorry." But he gets up and he decides that he's going to be a hard-on because he was watching the whole purse thing and there's this electricity in the air and, you know, fights break out all the time *at* other fights. I mean just because everyone just gets so amped. It's like a spark from a fire. I've seen it before. Especially with girl fights for some reason.

Now, I already bought these other guys drinks but I offer to get him one but he tells me no: "I want money," he says. I just start laughing at him. And all these people just jump on him. He was making a big show out of "Hold me back, hold me back" but everyone there seemed to know that if he was let go he was going to get his ass kicked. I mean I'm not a big guy, I'm 175, but this guy is smaller than me. Meanwhile I'm having to hold back the first guy I almost got into a fight with because now he's my new best pal. He wants to kick this guy's ass.

It doesn't seem like there's an overriding message here, though, is there?
Well, it's better to walk away, I think, but just because I'm a pacifist doesn't mean I have no responsibility to prevent harm: a woman that's getting her ass kicked . . . you know . . . I'm not a eunuch.

Do you have these like Vietnam screaming nightmares?
No. Well, I had nightmares for a long time, though. Definitely. Not now, though. I was very nervous, though, and my girlfriend at the time couldn't sleep. I'd wake up at nighttime and she'd be crying. It was hard.

Do you think it had anything to do with the end of your relationship with her?
[Pause] Might have. It's hard to separate out that stuff, though. From my perspective it seemed to strengthen our connections to each other because it created a bond. Maybe like going to war with somebody. So if she wants to run off and get married to my best friend, well, screw it, she's entitled to some slack, because she went through a lot.

THE PLACES TO LIVE MOST LIKELY TO GET YOU THE KIND OF FIGHTS YOU SO ARDENTLY DESIRE: TO THE DEATH!

Sure, sure there are some Johnny-come-latelies that you may try to argue ON the list (Sudan, Rwanda) but the following list was compiled after carefully culling State Department travel advisories and looking at stats going a few years back that were connected to violent crimes, and the kind of interpersonal struggle that really is momentously measurable: loss of life.

So for a vacation test of your ULTIMATE skills may we invite you to peruse the possibility of sudden death in these fine vacation hot spots. Leave your troubles at home. And bring lots of cash.

1. Angola
2. The Balkans
3. Colombia
4. Côte D'Ivoire
5. India
6. Indonesia
7. Iraq
8. Israel
9. Nigeria
10. Pakistan
11. The Philippines
12. South Africa
13. United States
14. Uzbekistan
15. Venezuela
16. Zimbabwe

FOURTEEN

I, SOCCER HOOLIGAN!

There's Third World chaos. Nothing beats Third World chaos if chaos is what you want. The analogy might be going crazy in a crazy house. When the law, as it was, never existed except as some sort of weird schema of wild jungle hate, then moving beyond it seems to be so easy. Will we ever get out of the Middle Eastern morass? Will Africa ever be a continent *not* beset with woe? Will crypto-narco death squads never cease fighting over Central American cocaine profits?

Who cares?

If you live in a place where you can sleep at night with a reasonable expectation of waking up *without* a yawning head wound, then it's probably okay to tender a guess that you don't. If, in fact, you do care, your armchair politicking is probably just a salve designed to soothe your sense of sorrow over greasing your larders with layer upon layer of filthy lucre. Because, you see, it seems that here in the First World our concerns are much more provincial and we get our chaos in small slices: movies, Eminem CDs, and role-playing games that occasionally break through the skin of gross irreality in a place like Columbine or Virginia Tech and shock everybody for a few minutes before we all go back to meditating on beauty queens strangled in sex shockers and variously instructive dating do's and don'ts from Hollywood's drama club.

But when you're comparing apples and apples, things start to make much more sense. First World chaos is its own piquant blend of ghetto fights, drive-by shootings, and trailer-park-backyard-meth-fueled wrestling matches. And while the deceptively placid suburban idyll of South Central Los Angeles or the despairing post-industrialism of a Detroit seem to all point down the same road, why is it that nowhere outside of Russia, with its barely First World wiles, do I feel more in real physical peril than I do when I'm in the UK?

Well, let's go to the UK to find out.

Pete the Boxer promised an underground fight match à la Guy Ritchie's walk on the wild side in his pre–Mr. Madonna flick *Snatch*. In four days I might be able to make £4,000, which, given how execrably the US dollar is doing these

days, is real goddamned cash. The way it works is this: it's tournament style and the touts, the degenerate gamblers, pays their money and they takes their chances. The more you fight and win, the more you make. Rules seem pretty nonexistent but while takedowns are fine, I am told if I start doing any "chokey ground shit you might find your hands full." As we sit sipping at the Buffalo Bar in Islington, Pete has led me to believe, through a casual semaphore of nods, smiles, and raised eyebrows, this would mean fighting much more than other fighters. One on one. So I nod assent and he moves to make a call.

But first a drink. And another. And another. And pretty soon he starts thinking he'll come out of retirement, especially since the East End cats who set him up still owe him. And while I try to send him off to his call like Chamberlain, he gets there as Churchill and queers the whole deal, especially since the deal never included him threatening to cut ANYONE'S balls off. Maybe it's the veneer of politesse that seems to mask a virulent and big-balled unhealthiness that always fools me, but the Brits are clearly, by my Western standards, insane. I've been here one day and the whole of late summertime London feels like one group of people running from one fight to the next. Maybe it's the national dipsomania, who knows? But I've gone 6,000 miles and have nothing to show for it. No fight, no fight that'll pay £4,000, no interview with Lee Murray, no nothing outside of a bit of nightclub conviviality.

Until I meet Jack Sargeant, and, like some sort of Grimm's fairy-tale character, he says, "How now, brown cow? Why so glum?" And I explain my plight, and he offers like some sort of magical-bean-toting fairy, a solution: Would a soccer hooligan do you for?

What? You mean he likes soccer? And drinking? And running from the cops? Sounds like Tuesday in Naples.
And he proceeds to explain to me that his friend recently had his door kicked in by the police or Interpol or Scotland Yard or some such fucking thing and they seized his computers, which were chockfull of fight plans, train and game schedules, pics of fights, and his manuscript on precisely this: soccer violence. All gone now, in the hands of the authorities, who had identified him as someone involved in "a conspiracy to commit violent disorder."

And so he asks again: You wanna talk to him?

Oh yeah. Ladies and gentlemen: Lorne Brown, soccer hooligan.
Actually the correct term would be football hooligan—not soccer—or football casual.

Okay. I stand corrected. So what's your team? Which is really for me like asking what's your favorite cricket team? I have no fucking idea really. But there are some that might, so go ahead and tell me.

Brighton and Hove Albion, who are based in Brighton, south coast of England. Then Millwall for three seasons when I was banned by the courts and club. I actually don't go at the moment as I'm banned again. But I followed them from 1987 onward all over the country. You know, originally I started going FOR the football but soon got swept up in the whole atmosphere and started going more for the action than the game. But I was still passionate about supporting the club.

This seems like a roughly agreed upon deal, yeah? Are there markers like there used to be in skinhead culture that follows the football hooligan? Braces up? Braces down? That kind of thing?

The "casuals," as football hooligans became known in the 1980s, wore certain clothes to blend in with the crowds, away from the old skinhead image. We wore labels such as Armani, Lacoste, Italian sportswear like Fila, Kappa, and wore Adidas trainers and Timberland boots. It became just as important to look good.

Now, is it a fight-on-sight deal? Or are you more likely to fight with fans from some teams more than with others?

It wouldn't be random violence. You would know who the opposition was by the way they were dressed. The Firms, as they were known as, would try and meet anywhere in the town where the game was being played, away from the police, if possible. And there are old rivalries too, such as Millwall and West Ham, Manchester United and Leeds United, and these would attract thousands of hooligans. With Brighton it was mainly geographical, and so our rivals are Crystal Palace. Portsmouth. Oxford United and Leyton Orient. These games could be very violent: the last time we played Crystal Palace we took four hundred lads to their ground and it took 250 police to prevent a riot.

Have the precautions they've taken to keep you all from traveling worked?

The police tactics have worked very well at home and abroad. The use of CCTV [closed-circuit television] cameras on helmets, helicopters, riot police, dogs, mounted police, and heavy jail sentences have deterred a lot of people, but for big games everyone still turns out for the day.

What was the deal with the police seizing all of your stuff?

Well, I'd been arrested several times for fighting. And had been to court a few times over the years so the police knew who I was, along with many of the others in the Firm. They have what they call an intelligence officer assigned to each club to identify hooligans. So one Saturday we played Leeds United and there was trouble involving forty fans fighting in a pub and in the street in one of Brighton's main roads. Later fifty of us clashed in another pub in the historical part of town about ten o'clock in the evening. Ten thousand pounds' worth of damage was done and several people injured and a police dog was killed in the fighting when the police tried to break it up. Unfortunately for me and twenty others it was caught on CCTV. This led to our houses being targeted, riot police kicking our doors down and arresting most of us. I was lucky they just seized all my equipment and later dropped the charges of conspiracy to commit violent disorder. Ten others were not so lucky and were sent to jail. Hence, I've kept my head down as I have a three-year-old son now. Which means I choose my games very wisely now.

Is there any sort of history to this violence? I mean, were they doing this shit back in the 1920s?

It's been going on in one way or another for a hundred years, but it wasn't until the 1970s that it became organized and almost fashionable for a while. In the 1940s a hand grenade was thrown onto the pitch at a Millwall game. And the two main Scottish clubs, Glasgow Rangers and Celtic, have been fighting over football and religion since the game began. It has died down a bit now due to police efforts and heavy punishments in the courts. But in the '70s, thousands would try and take each other's stands in pitched battles, and they would fight it out on the pitch with the game still going ahead.

Do chicks fight as well?

Never seen it myself but have heard of it on rare occasions.

Are the clubs multicultural? You know, bringing together different races and colors and creeds in a veritable festival of fighting brotherhood?

It's mainly white and working-class. Between the ages of fifteen and fifty. However, some clubs such as Birmingham are known as the Zulus due to the large number of black lads in their Firm. In fact, the Zulus usually feature in the top five worst hooligan gangs in the country and have been responsible for some of the worst violence seen at matches over the years. Most Firms do have some lads from other ethnic backgrounds, though.

How come there was no trouble when the World Cup was played in the UK the last time?

That one's simple: England didn't qualify for the World Cup then. In 1994 we were knocked out by Holland in Rotterdam in the group stages in 1993. I was there and it was insane before the game and after, with over fifteen hundred arrests as England fans rioted.

Is there anything that comes close to the thrill of a good fight? And are there techniques for doing better in these fights that maybe a trained fighter would not have even thought of?

Nothing else gives you that surge of adrenaline that you get just before a fight. It can't be explained. Addictive? Yes. And the camaraderie, being in a tight spot and having to fight your way out? You can't replace it with anything else. And I don't think a jiu-jitsu fighter would stand any better chance in these fights than anyone else as they are mainly gang related, and although he could take most of them down one on one, he would be swamped after a while. We had kickboxers and boxers in our Firm, and as tough as these guys were there wasn't much call for technique in these situations.

So what is going on, technique-wise?

It's pretty much anything goes: punching, kicking, head butts, the lot. However, kicking people on the ground is usually frowned upon, although it does go on as some people take things a bit far, and there have been several deaths over the years. But I've been in fights where we have been attacked with flare guns, CS [2-Chlorobenzalmalononitrile], or teargas and knives. Although never guns. Not from football fans, that is. Knives were used a lot more in the 1980s, especially Stanley knives. I've never carried a weapon myself. Just not my thing. However, I have used umbrellas, bottles, planks of wood, and used a cop's stick on him once.

www.acasuallook.co.uk

THE DIRTY DOZEN:

BEST NORTH AMERICAN SPORTS BRAWLS AND OUR UNFLINCHINGLY UNREPENTANT TAKE ON WHY THEY WERE GREAT

Houston Rockets vs. Los Angeles Lakers, December 9, 1977—Kermit Washington, sucker punch. Rudy Tomjanovich, hospitalization, attempted murder, career-ending injuries. 'Nuff said.

Tom Gamboa Gets Jumped, September 19, 2002—The 54-year-old Kansas City Royals coach Tom Gamboa gets attacked by a meth-fueled father and teenage son double team. Who said good parenting is dead? Outside of everyone who reads this story?

Los Angeles Dodgers vs. San Francisco Giants, August 22, 1965—Two intentional beanings, a Juan Marichal–launched bat to the head of Johnny Roseboro, and a perfectly wrist-slappish eight-game suspension. When they talked about the good ol' days . . . this is probably what they mean.

Montreal Canadiens vs. Boston Bruins, March 13, 1955—The best part of having control is losing it, and Canadiens legend Maurice Richard was never known for having much to begin with, so when he took a stick to Hal Laycoe—and almost everyone else who tried to stop him from taking a stick to Laycoe—he had clearly LOST it. For his troubles he was suspended by league president Clarence Campbell, who, at his next public appearance, was attacked in a riot that resulted in over half a million dollars of damage and the arrest of almost every single Richard fan in attendance.

Malice at the Palace: Indiana Pacers vs. Detroit Pistons, November 19, 2004—Everybody beating their chests over how "horrible," how "dreadful" a state of affairs basketball had degenerated to: whatever. If this wasn't the greatest game of basket-brawl you had ever seen, well, we'll jump out of the stands and start wildly punching almost everyone in sight. Sure, Artest was suspended for an entire season, and Stephen Jackson (30 games), and Jermaine O'Neal (25 games), but who cares? We value honesty over prime-time propriety. On display here was exactly what *should* happen when millionaires are toyed with by the great unwashed: ass-kicking.

Milbury vs. The Shoe, December 23, 1979—Boston Bruin Mike Milbury beat a cursing, kicking, stick-wielding fan with the fan's own shoe? Perfect.

Frank Francisco vs. A Woman's Nose, September 13, 2004—For the record? Her husband was a heckler, she aided and abetted the public decline of manners, Texas Rangers pitcher Francisco was just doing what anyone who reads Miss Manners would have known was exactly the right thing: he bust her in the nose with a folding chair. Life lesson learned? You will get suspended for fifteen games, get arrested, and plead no contest to misdemeanor assault charges. Oh, and you'll get sued and settle. Veeerrrrryyyy disappointing.

San Diego Padres vs. Atlanta Braves, August 12, 1984—Nineteen ejected players, five spectators arrested, Braves manager Joe Torre pegging San Diego manager Dick Williams as Hitler in a baseball cap. America's pastime? You know it, baby.

Brooklyn Dodgers fan vs. George Magerkurth, September 19, 1940—Enraged parole violater Frank Germano leaps out of the stands to whale on the former heavyweight-boxer-turned-umpire Magerkurth whose call cost Brooklyn first place, handing it to the Cincinnati Reds. Gave new life to the phrase "Kill the umpire!"

Mike Tyson vs. Evander Holyfield, June 28, 1997—C'mon? Ear avulsion? An ensuing riot? Tooth-based mayhem? The last great thing that Tyson ever did, which just about says it all.

The Punch-up in Piestany: Canada vs. Soviet Union, World Junior Hockey Championships, January 5, 1987—Bench-clearing brawls that saw EVERYONE in the arena fighting. Panicked officials turned off the lights in a sad attempt to restore order: EVERYONE kept fighting in the dark. Game canceled, both teams banned from the tournament. An amazing think-tank level of commitment to the fistic arts. Kudos, gentlemen.

Riddick Bowe vs. Andrew Golota, July 11, 1996—Low blows and a head butt disqualified the "Polish Prince." When a member of the Brooklyn-born Bowe's entourage attacked Golota, smashing him in the head with a walkie-talkie, the ensuing rumble in the ring led to fans brawling in the stands at Madison Square Garden, ending, not so predictably, in a riot. Now THAT'S entertainment.

THE BRAWLING HALL OF FAME FOR NO PARTICULAR REASON

BILLY MARTIN: For being drunk. And fighting. And fighting drunk.

THE CITY of BOSTON: For the same reasons.

TY COBB: For beating up a one-armed man with his one fake arm.

JAKE LA MOTTA: For having great peripheral vision, which was the key to his un-knock-outability.

KYLE FARNSWORTH and BILL ROMANOWSKI: Are they not one and the same person?

MIKE TYSON: WAR at the STORE. Case closed.

And last but not least . . .

JIM BROWN: Do NOT, we repeat NOT, play golf with this man. Or let's put it another way: Is an eagle worth your life?

FIFTEEN

HOLIDAY ON ICE,

OR, WHAT TO DO WHEN CONFRONTED BY AN ANGRY CANADIAN WITH A STICK

Hockey's become sort of a backwater. This happens when strikes drag on for years, when rule changes change an already difficult game to follow, and when the public's taste for and confusion regarding thuggery reigns supreme. And that goddamned video of Steve Moore's head bouncing off the ice like a handball with hair every time someone wanted to talk about hockey didn't help either.

But there WAS a time, a time before the time when the WNBA was scoring more viewers than NHL hockey (and there'll be no claims made for hockey here as its reputation as "soccer on ice" has not been lost on us) when some of the toughest men ever to clock time in a sanctioned sports event plied their trade. That trade being, specifically: hockey enforcer.

Part shark, part hitman, the enforcer was an indispensable component of the iced trade, and though grace-note suspensions were routinely handed out by way of "penalty minutes," the tough guy, make that TOUGH guy, as sports hero hadn't had this kind of juice since Ty Cobb was beating up people in the stands for heckling him.

Of the assembled TOUGH guys, whose reputations rest upon weeks and weeks of penalty minutes, a few names emerge, but only ONE name emerges as the toughest AND the best: TIE DOMI.

Domi, with more penalty minutes than any other player in the history of the Toronto Maple Leafs, was third overall in career NHL penalty minutes (see sidebar, pages 199–201). Which means that after a sixteen-year career (that just ended in 2006) and over 1,000 games, he's gotten into more fights than probably just about anyone else you KNOW. On ice. Against guys with sticks. BIGGER guys with sticks.

Which is precisely why he's here.

Hockey fights: bullshit attempt at pandering to a sensation-mad fan base (and we're OKAY with that) or something else?

Tie Domi: Hockey's a game of a lot of emotion but inside all of that emotion is a game where occasionally you got a guy who wants to take a cheap shot. Or a liberty. Whatever you want to call it. And usually there's a guy or two whose job it is to respond to that. To make the guy's cheap shot cost a little bit. At the very least he's there to RESPOND to it. It's not the case that you get the better of him but at least somebody's holding somebody accountable. So when you have a tough guy on the bench it makes guys respect what's going on a lot more because they know they're going to be held accountable.

And, you know, sometimes fights don't always happen to get someone back. Sometimes it's to change the flow of the game. If you're down 2-0 you gotta change something. If you're not in the mood, you still gotta do it to turn the game around. And that's what I was best at. And I'd go after one of their best players to get someone to come at me. Or I would yap at the bench. You do this long enough and you know someone's going to come. But because I was one of the tougher guys, people didn't want to go with me, but even if they came up to me just to talk, if the opportunity was right? I'd do it. And everybody knew if I did it when we were down I was doing it for the team and not just for myself. But guys who are enforcers are born into this role. No coach is creating a personality that can get out there and do this stuff.

What about these super highly publicized things like Todd Bertuzzi? (Steve Moore suffered three fractured vertebrae in his neck, a grade-three concussion, vertebral ligament damage, stretching of the brachial plexus nerves, and facial cuts at the hands of Bertuzzi.)

Moore should have seen it coming. Look, Moore hit Markus Naslund, putting him out for three games. The best player on the Vancouver Canucks. And he's the captain. So when Moore hit him he had to know that next game he was a target. Bertuzzi's not a tough guy. Neither is Moore actually, but if you play hockey you know someone's coming for you. And everybody was trying to do something to try to fight him and he wouldn't respond, right? Unfortunately when Bertuzzi got him his head hit the ice, BUT he shoulda seen it coming. And because he shoulda seen it coming, he, first shift, shoulda fought somebody just to get it over with. Instead he was just acting like he was going to get away with it but that's just not the way the game's played. And the game's been played for how many years? I don't know what kind of fucking hockey HE was watching as a kid but last time I checked if you take out the other team's best player with a dirty hit you better be expecting to answer the bell.

All right, fight techniques? What are the ones that I can use to keep from getting Steve Moore'd?

The most important ones are having the right balance, being on top of your feet, and having a good grip. If your legs are not squared properly and you don't have a good grip, you're going to have a tough time. I was always the smaller guy…

At 5'10, 210?

If you're fighting guys 6'5' and 235, yeah. But the thing I got to tell you is this: if you don't like getting hit you might as well not do the role. You don't like fighting? Don't start, because once you fight a few guys you're always going to be known as a guy who'll fight. But I'd grab the guy's shirt, right underneath his chin, and I used to bring it, I used to throw pretty hard, but I'd bring it from what they called the South Pole. And I used to throw that with my chin down to

protect my face. After that I'd just follow my hand because I knew somewhere in there, between my two fists was going to be his face. So whatever hand I'm throwing, I turn my chin the same way. (For all you fight fans, turning his head to the right if he was throwing punches with his right.)

Grabbing the jersey is important too. You've got to grab a guy on the jersey or jacket or something by the elbow or further down the arm. Some guys grab right underneath the armpit and they get tagged. But you grab at the elbow or down toward the hand the guy can't throw a punch. You also gotta lock your arm. If you lock your arm straight when you grab the guy you can hold him and it's tough to break away from that.

I *invented* the little jab punch with the jersey. Like I said, I'd grab the guy's jersey right under his chin. These shirts DO stretch so if you pull it out and throw that little punch with the hand that's grabbing the jersey you can really actually hurt a guy. Really make his eyes water. Add to that The Spin. I started spinning guys to get them off balance. That's probably my trademark too, but once I got the spin going they knew I was kinda in control. If you spin toward the arm they're throwing, you're walking right into it, so I'd spin away from the punch.

Okay—jersey grab, chin punches, The Spin, head toward punching arm, and blind punches in the vicinity of the jersey hand. This shit work on the street? I mean, with any sort of regularity?

Oh yeah. You know I didn't take any shit from anybody but when I was in New York it happened a lot. People'd see me at a bar and they'd say, "Hey, you're Tie Domi!" And then after a few drinks it'd be, "Oh, you're not that big, Domi." A few more drinks later it'd be, "You probably ain't that tough, either." And then finally it'd be something like, "Nice haircut, asshole." And before you know it the guy's staring at the ceiling, laying on his back. One time in Chicago a couple of Marines were in my face. They'd been bothering my teammates and so I asked, "Is there a problem here?" The guy gets in my face, nose to nose like he's a drill sargeant, "PARDON ME, SIR, WHAT DID YOU SAY, SIR?" And I said, "Hey, buddy, get outta my face right now or I'll put you in a coma." I grabbed them both by the throat and threw them down the stairs. I took care of my teammates on and off the ice.

Okay . . . and finally, coming from a tough guy, this might mean something: name some of the toughest guys you've ever fought . . .

In no particular order

1. **Bob Probert, for sure.** "We had some dandies. I was young and playing at Madison Square Garden and that's when I used to do that WWE shit: miming the champion's belt, the speed bag, and all of that shit. [Mark] Messier convinced me to stop that, though."

2. **Dave Brown**

3. **Donald Brashear**

4. **Craig "The Chief" Berube**

5. **Ken Baumgartner**

6. **Joe Kocur**

7. **Chris Simon**

8. **Rob Ray**

9. **Ken Daneyko**

   and last but not least

10. **Tony Twist**

TOP TEN CAREER NHL PENALTY MINUTE LEADERS

	MINUTES	YEARS PLAYED

1. Dave "Tiger" Williams   3,966   1974–1988

TEAMS Maple Leafs, Canucks, Red Wings, Kings, Whalers

"NOTABLE" ACHIEVEMENTS Spent the equivalent of over seventy complete games in the penalty box during his career, and was once involved in a stick duel with Dave Hutchinson of the LA Kings—while IN the penalty box.

2. Dale Hunter   3,565   1980–1999

TEAMS Nordiques, Capitals, Avalanche

"NOTABLE" ACHIEVEMENTS When his number was retired by Washington he was presented with his own penalty box.

	MINUTES	YEARS PLAYED

3. Tie Domi   3,515   1989–2006

TEAMS Rangers, Jets, Maple Leafs

"NOTABLE" ACHIEVEMENTS Sprayed a heckling fan with water while in the penalty box in Philadelphia. A drunk fan banged on the glass until the panel gave way, causing the fan to fall into the box with Domi, who got in his whacks before the fan was ejected from the arena.

4. Marty McSorley   3,381   1983–2000

TEAMS Penguins, Oilers, Kings, Rangers, Sharks, Bruins

"NOTABLE" ACHIEVEMENTS Convicted for assaulting Donald Brashear with his stick (Brashear fell backward to the ice and received a concussion), suspended for a year, never played another game in the NHL.

5. Bob Probert   3,300   1985–2002

TEAMS Red Wings, Blackhawks

"NOTABLE" ACHIEVEMENTS Once arrested for cocaine possession while crossing the Detroit-Windsor border, was jailed, suspended from the NHL. He was banned from traveling with the Red Wings to any games in Canada for over two seasons. Heeyyy . . . who among us . . . ?

6. Rob Ray   3,207   1989–2004

TEAMS Sabres, Senators

"NOTABLE" ACHIEVEMENTS Ray's fighting style was to remove his helmet, pads, and jersey, giving his opponents nothing to grab onto. The NHL created additional penalties for those who did this, and it became known as the Rob Ray Rule.

7. Craig "The Chief" Berube

3,149   1986–2003

TEAMS Flyers, Maple Leafs, Flames, Capitals, Islanders

"NOTABLE" ACHIEVEMENTS Suspended for one game without pay for calling Peter Worrell, one of the few African-Americans in the NHL, a "monkey" during an on-ice scrap. Berube himself is a Native American. He's lucky he didn't get scalped…

8. Tim Hunter

3,142   1981–1997

TEAMS Flames, Nordiques, Canucks, Sharks

"NOTABLE" ACHIEVEMENTS Possibly the best hockey fighter of all time, pound-for-pound, and best technical fighter, according to hockeyfights.com.

9. Chris "Knuckles" Nilan

3,043   1979–1992

TEAMS Canadiens, Bruins, Rangers

"NOTABLE" ACHIEVEMENTS Holds the record for highest average penalty minutes per game (4.42) and single-game penalty minute record (42).

10. Rick Tocchet

2,970   1984–2002

TEAMS Flyers, Penguins, Kings, Bruins, Capitals, Coyotes

"NOTABLE" ACHIEVEMENTS One of only four players in NHL history with over 400 goals *and* 2,000 penalty minutes, he pleaded guilty to his involvement in a sports gambling ring along with a New Jersey state trooper and Wayne Gretzky's wife.

Note that well-known goons Dave "The Hammer" Schultz (the poster boy for the "Broad Street Bullies" Flyers teams of the 1970s) is number 34 on the list, and Stu "The Grim Reaper" Grimson (possibly the best hockey goon nickname ever) is number 41. To Schultz's credit, he also owns, by a wide margin, the single-season record for penalty minutes with 472. To see these guys in action, check out YouTube.com.

THE BEST DOCUMENTARY THAT DOESN'T MAKE YOU FEEL LIKE YOU WANT TO WEAR A BERET & MOVE TO FRANCE AND FEATURES TOOTHLESS MEN SAVAGELY BEATING EACH OTHER TO A PULP WHILE WEARING ICE SKATES

The Chiefs (2005) Directed by Jason Gileno

You know who Wayne Gretzky is? No? Okay, what about Bobby Hull? No? Jesus, what about that Paul Newman movie *Slapshot* then? Okay, that's ringing some bells, right? A ragtag band of hockey degenerates and their lucky, plucky story of pugilistic perseverance, sort of a *Bad News Bears* but instead of lovable kids and Jodie Foster, you get toothless Canadians who like to fight? Well, you know how every fiction is based on some kind of reality? Well, this *is* that reality. And though reality TV has poisoned the well of well-turned documentaries, this one does what good ones are supposed to do: sits back and follows its characters through their unexpectedly complicated lives (versus leading its "actors" through completely unbelievable cons). And it's these real lives that make this a sort of compelling look at hockey (which we have a hard time seeing anyone not Canadian or living West of the continental divide giving a shit about) a really compelling look at combat. You know the old joke about going to a fight and having a hockey game break out? *The Chiefs* IS that joke, and more than funny, it's a solid technical primer on fighting on ice skates, and a celebration and quiet embrace of the elemental nature of competition, while its raw ballet makes you forget that hockey is just about the most boring game ever. More watch-able than a biathlon, and better fights too.

SIXTEEN

I STOOP TO CONQUER

CHRIS SANFORD'S FOND REMINISENCE OF KNOCKING OUT EUGENE ROBINSON, BRINGING IN THE DEAD POST-KATRINA & OTHER GENERALIZED TALES OF DOUBLE-FISTED DERRING-DO . . .

It was like the Fourth of July. There was a silvery burst of light and then ease. And quiet. A tremendous ease. The mat was cool against my face, and as unseen hands lifted me upright I heard myself murmur. Almost whisper even, "I'm okay. I slipped. I tripped." And because these unseen hands—now seen, but whose owners are unknown to me—believe me, they let me go, and down I go again. And again there's the intrusion of hands and I feel like someone who's had a nap interrupted. Twice. And so, more forcefully this time, "I'm *fine*. I *tripped*." And my legs are unsteady under me and someone makes me watch what just happened, or rather, the video of what just happened, and I can see that I've been knocked out. Or abducted by aliens for all I know. In any case, I was out. No more than ten seconds, but clearly out, out for what felt like a lot longer than ten seconds.

I was in Fight Club SF and I had been knocked out by a pro, Chris Sanford. And later in some cagefight in Fresno I run into him again backstage, immediately before he goes out and submits with an armbar a cat named Jack Cardenas. And then again and again: in Las Vegas, in LA, in bars here, there, and everywhere. His name keeps coming up and eventually he's on TV, the first season of *The Ultimate Fighter* TV show.

Now, I'd been knocked DOWN before but never knocked OUT, and of course never knocked out by someone so goddamned ubiquitous, and in being knocked out I had never guessed that the first and most definitive missile delivered to thems that would have it delivered no other way would be so life-changing. Once you've been knocked out you fight differently. You fight like someone who then fully takes fighting now, finally and in good measure, seriously. I'm not saying that you win any more than you did before. I'm just saying that you're finally willing to die trying, and this can make all the difference in the world for some men. Or for me, at the very least. And so in the name of closure, um, redemption, and, ultimately, revenge, I seek him out to find out if it was as good for him as it was for me.

Now, did it feel as good to knock me out as I think it'd be for me to knock *you* out?
He laughs and shrugs his shoulders "Hey, man. No. I felt bad. I didn't want to fight anybody that night."

But you knew the rules, everybody had to fight.
Well, I had never been there before that night, so I thought I could just watch and check it out. But you came over and said something like, "C'mon, let's fight." And I tried to beg off and you asked again and, so I said, "Okay."

Do you remember what happened after that?
Yeah. You kicked the fuck out of me and that's when I said "Okay" for the second time, and you came in with your hands a little low and that was it.

Well, not to make any excuses . . . but if I had known you were a pro I would have been a LOT more cautious. You said you hadn't trained before.
"Did I? I don't remember saying that." And he doesn't say it but he doesn't have to say it because I've already shamed myself enough by even bringing it up. Rule Number 478: If you got your ass kicked, do not equivocate around the ass-kicking.

And what did you all do after that?

Well, you challenged me again. And I beat you again.

You didn't knock me out again!

No. I tapped you out with a choke. I felt bad about that too, because you were in NO shape to go again, but you kept challenging me.

And I could repeat this sad mockery, making sound bite after sound bite, and it'd tell you the same thing in the same way, a way that would not and could not be changed. Ever. I had gotten my ass kicked. And then I had gone back and got my ass kicked again. And it was pretty clear I'd have gone back as many times as I could to get it kicked as many times as I could before I'd give over to the understanding that I wasn't going to win this one.

But what of Sanford? Known was the fact that he had moved into sports management and had recently started tooling around town in a Benz, an expensive one, and that he had had some mortgage business or some such thing as well. Would he be interviewed?

We going to spend much time talking about me knocking you out?

Uh, no. I mean, whatever you want.

Good. You know what was wild, though? All of that shit that went down in New Orleans.

Is the water so hot it is cold, or so cold it is hot? I mean, is there something going on in post-Katrina Louisiana that I had missed? . . . You were there?

Yeah. Steel sent me there.

And then the scales started falling away in big ol' chunks from my eyes. You see, the Steel Foundation was like the defunct Sandline International. Or KBR. Ringing any bells for you? Supplier of "contractors" for corporate contracts. Be it in Iraq, Central America, or, I guess in this instance, southern states America. They usually draw their employee base from the ranks of the formerly ranked: SEALs, Rangers, and so on. Sanford was in the service?

Um . . .

It signaled a pause, a pause that I had heard before when I've asked CIA guys stuff that was politically inopportune for me to have asked. So I asked it again: Were you in the service?

Yeah. I was in the army.

And they sent you to New Orleans?

No. Steel sent me. All of the large hoteliers wanted to secure their properties, up to and including their employees, who it was felt may have been in some sort of peril. I mean, no one knew, right? So I got the call and signed on. I was supposed to be there for ninety days, but after about fifteen, I said, "So long. I'm leaving." It was crazy, dude.

I thought a lot of that so-called craziness had been debunked as never having happened.

Bullshit. It was sheer lunacy. We pulled some guy off of a roof. We did this extraction, you know, rappel in and we get this fool and he's shooting at rescue workers and so we get him and I asked him, "Why the fuck were you shooting at the rescue workers?" And you know what he said to me? "Because they had a green boat." A GREEN BOAT. This is not what was written about.

Isn't it lovely what happens when the old laws and then even convention cease having any sort of meaning anymore?

Actually, no. It's not. It was fucked up. I was THERE at the Superdome and I saw credible proof of instances where one woman had been raped several times. I was watching them stack bodies. We were drawing and returning fire . . . fighting from block to block . . .

What? Who? How?

He shrugged his shoulders slowly. "We never knew. And here's something else that wasn't reported, and that's that while we were totally vested up, armed, and equipped, we weren't the only ones there. I remember once we came across these guys lifting luxury cars off of one of our parking lots and I go up and say, 'Excuse me. What are you guys doing?' And right away they're drawing on me and my guys are drawing on them and I'm like 'Whoa, whoa, wait, we don't need to fight. We just need to see some ID.' And they showed us something and . . ."

Who were they?

"They were cops." And he smiled. "Hey. I don't know. They said they were afraid looters were going to get their cars, or something, so they were loading them onto some commandeered truck. But there were like gangs. Gangs of guys outside of the random crazies. Random crazies don't steal forklifts, okay. They shoot green boats. Forklifts were stolen to yank up security gates. Gun stores were empty. But gangs just descended on the city from Mississippi and wherever and were stealing a lot more than the beer they were showing you on TV. We chased some Vietnam vet through the halls of one of the hotels we were securing. It was full-on Rambo shit. He had gotten one of our radios and gotten on our channel and so he was one step ahead of us always. Besides, we knew he knew some shit because he was making no mistakes when we were making sweeps."

How'd you know he was a vet?

Well, we found his diary at one point. And IT was crazy. And full of crazy shit. We never caught him, though. He was good.

So, it sounds sort of like merc heaven. Why'd you leave?

"I could make $180K easily going to Iraq right now, but I'm not too interested in doing that, either. Life's too short and the fight game's keeping me busy here and sooo . . ." He trails off. "But I left New Orleans because there was no way it was going to be controlled. I had shit for local staff. I told one guy to do something and he told me, 'Where I'm from in Mississippi, we don't have uppity niggers talking to good white folks like that.' Keep in mind, as his boss I had asked him something real basic: 'Please wake up and do your job.' I had guys posing with high-powered firearms on the top of cars. There was just no way to control the place and there was no sign at all that there would be. So you get tired of having the bad guys shooting at you, the good guys shooting at you, and the crazy guys shooting at you. So fuck that. I left. Steel was pretty unhappy with me, but I was pretty happy to be out of there."

We were standing at a local cage-fight event, more visible now since California's athletic commission okayed mixed martial arts sporting events statewide. The PA was pumping that kind of generic angry-guy music that's the perpetual soundtrack for monster truck events, while high-channeled ginch flowed by on heels with either too much, or the wrong kind of, attitude. Damien Noorkabash, CEO of fightwear gear company Konjo was there, Sal Russo from Cesar Gracie's fight team was there, and someone finally said, amid talk of matchups, rematches, and potential matches, "Ah, these'll be some good fights."

Undoubtedly.

ACKNOWLEDGMENTS

Some of this writing in other forms has appeared in Vice, the Violence Issue (November 2002), and *Grappling* magazine. Invaluable assistance was also offered by gentleman and scholar Todd Hester, editor nonpareil Doug Grad, Kjetil Kausland, Gabriella Marks/www.triggerfinger.com, Lorne Brown/www.acasuallook.co.uk, Christian Anthony/www.theoxbow.com/musicforadults, Dr. Steve G. Ballinger, Tie Domi, Kevin Weeks, Joe Donnelly, Mike Gavin, Todd Conner, and finally Vinnie Rose/www.skullgame.com.

Photo editor: Gabriella Marks
Illustrations: [On *The Punchline...*] Michael Manning/www.thespidergarden.net; Pilar Newton, and Abram Hall.

Photo credits for *FIGHT*: Pages ii, vi, 3, 21–23, 92–100, 118, 119, 121, 124, 155, 157, 159, 162, 164, 166–68, Todd Hester; 4, Richard Morganstern; 8, Christian Anthony; 10, M. Gallagher; 12, Mike Hadley; 16, Lorcan Otway; 19, Eugene Robinson; 25, Columbia Pictures/SONY; 30, Kjetil Kausland; 31, 33, Richard Corman; 38–39, 127, Gabriella Marks; 46, 109, Associated Press; 56, Courtesy of James Painter; 71, Alexa DeGennaro; 74, Sheryl Perlow; 76–78, Michael Manning; 80, 82, Sandy Sokolowski; 87, Pilar Newton; 101, Courtesy of Karl Gotch; 105, 107, Courtesy of Gene LeBell; 130, 134, 152, 188, 197, Getty Images; 136, Don Smith; 141, Abram Hall; 154, Sotaro Shinoda; 182, 185, 186, Lorne Brown; 190, Hank Olen/New York Daily News; 194, 199, Wes Strome; 196, Damian Strohmeyer/Sports Illustrated; 206, Luke Sonnier; 209, Pat Moriarity